KINGPIN LANDLORD

Unlocking the Secrets to Real Estate Investing

SCOTT ABERNATHY, MPM, RMP, GRI

TABLE OF CONTENTS

INTRODUCTION

*T*here are many reasons to own a rental home. Some folks may have owned a personal residence and were forced to move due to a job transfer, health problems, or a multitude of other personal reasons. When they decide to sell, they discover that they will need to write a five-digit check because the house isn't worth as much as it used to be and the closing costs plus the amount owed on the mortgage exceed the market value of the property.

Others may be novice investors who desire real estate in their portfolio. They understand the benefits — from cash flow to tax deductions — that rental properties have to offer. Real estate can be a great way to diversify your investments, and it can be an excellent hedge against inflation.

Then there are the professional investors. Those who own tens, hundreds, or even thousands of units. Some homes you may trade or flip. And others you keep depending on profitability. Even for professional investors, there are some houses with which you just get stuck.

Finally, there are those who haven't even invested in their first property yet. I applaud would-be investors for getting as much information as they can before they jump in the business. If I had followed my own advice, my learning curve would have looked more like a train track instead of the cracked Liberty Bell. Keep learning, but don't procrastinate. When you find a deal, it won't last long.

One thing that real estate investors have in common is they want to get as much out of their investment as possible. That is what I am going to discuss in this book. Get ready because some of this information will be counterintuitive. When I talk about getting top dollar for your rental home, I'm considering net dollars, not just the monthly rental income. For that matter, there are times when it is beneficial to take less than market value in rent. Several factors influence the profitability of a rental property, and frankly, what you rent it for is one of the least important.

In the meantime, I will discuss other things you can do to improve the bottom line. We will consider strategies for keeping good, long-term tenants by taking care of maintenance in a timely manner. I will explain the importance of conducting proper tenant screening in the first place to prevent you from losing your shirt in this business. And finally, we'll examine methods to help you obtain higher rental income.

It all boils down to the fact that owners must make sure their property is managed correctly. Landlording is a customer service business; if you don't take care of your customers (read tenants), you won't have them long. You must ensure you meet your customers' needs promptly, while at the same time not letting them take advantage of you.

With more than 30 years of experience renting scattered properties, mostly single-family homes, I have learned these techniques from many different sources. I owe a great deal to the National Association of Residential Property Managers, whose combined experience has kept me from making many mistakes. Their 6,000 members have proven to be a wealth of knowledge for me over the years. I learned many of the ideas in this book from one member or another, and then put them into practice in my company with excellent results. Following these strategies will dramatically increase your income.

I'll begin each chapter with a short story illustrating pitfalls you may encounter if your business is not attended to correctly. These tales are not meant to frighten you away from owning rental properties; they are only to emphasize the consequences of landlord errors. For the most part, if you run your business correctly, you will avoid most of these problems.

So let's get started on the way to making your rental home more profitable.

CHAPTER 1

TENANT SCREENING

*J*ohnny just bought his first rental house. It was in great shape, but empty and in need of a resident. The Realtor who sold it to him told him he should be able to fetch $1,000 a month. But, Johnny thought: Why not shoot for the moon? He placed an ad on Craigslist for $1,200 a month and waited for responses. Three weeks went by with only four calls and only one prospective tenant, who walked through it, turning her nose up the entire time.

With the first mortgage payment due in just a couple of days, Johnny began to feel a little desperate. He renewed his advertisement on Craigslist, noting its immediate availability. Later that day, Johnny received a call from a very sweet sounding lady named Rachael. Rachael explained that she and her family needed to move right away because their house had burned the night before. Johnny raced out to meet her at the property, lease in hand.

Rachael was an attractive woman in her mid-20s. She and Johnny hit it off right away. Opening the door, Johnny backed away and welcomed her into the small galley kitchen. Rachael loved the white cabinets, new carpet, patterned vinal floor and the smell of fresh paint. She stopped in the third bedroom and said, "This is perfect! What do I need to do to get it?"

"Well, I brought a lease with me," said Johnny, trying to hide his excitement. "We can do it today if you would like." He was envisioning making his payment and reaping long-term profits.

"That would be great!" said Racheal. "I'd love to have a place for my kids to go to bed tonight. Where do I sign?"

They went through the paperwork together and both signed on the dotted line.

"Okay, now with that done, all I need is to collect the security deposit and the first month's rent," Johnny said.

"Well, like I said, our house just burned down," Racheal explained. "Our insurance company is taking care of it, but the payment hasn't come yet. I am expecting the check any day. Would it be okay if I brought it to you when it comes?"

Johnny thought about it for only a second and said, "Sure, just let me know when it arrives, and I'll stop by and pick it up."

"Oh, thank you so much," Racheal said. "You've just made my day."

Reaching into his pocket, he grabbed the key. It still had the Real Estate Company's tag attached to it.

"Here's the key," he said. "It's the only one I have, so if you need more, feel free to make copies."

Rachael took the key with a big smile on her face. Later, Johnny realized her smile had reminded him of the Cheshire Cat's grin when he told Alice she was mad.

A few days went by and Johnny still had not heard from Rachael. He drove by the house to see if they were moving in okay. He noticed four cars parked in the driveway and along the road, all in some need of repair. There was a lot of milling around going on and Johnny just figured they were friends who were helping the unfortunate family who just lost their home move. Johnny did not want to bother them, so he didn't stop.

After several more days, Johnny still had not heard from his tenant, and he began to worry about his rent and security deposit. However, he hesitated to disturb his new tenants. After all, their house had just burned down.

"They surely don't need me burdening them any more than necessary," he thought. "Besides, Rachael said she would call when the check came."

By now, Johnny's first payment was late, but still within the grace period. He knew he had to pay it soon, so he picked up the phone and called Rachael.

"Hello?" said Racheal, sounding almost frantic.

"Hey Rachael, it's Johnny," he said. "I was wondering if your insurance company had paid your settlement yet."

"Oh my gosh!" she said. "You have no idea how difficult those insurance adjusters can be! They keep telling us it is on the way, but it never arrives. I promise I will let you know when it comes."

"Okay, just keep in mind that I need to make my house payment," said Johnny.

"Oh yes, of course," she replied. "I'll get it to you as soon as possible."

"Thanks so much," Johnny said as he heard the click of disconnection on the phone.

The rental house payment was due, so he wrote a check from his personal account to cover it. When Johnny's wife found out, she was upset.

"I thought you said this house was going to make money!" she yelled at him. Now, this was interfering with his personal life. He had to collect his rent.

It was now more than two weeks since Rachael and her family had moved into the house, so the next morning Johnny called his very past due tenant.

"The insurance company is giving us the runaround," Racheal explained. "My husband gets paid on Friday. We'll get it to you then."

"Friday is four days away," said Johnny. "The next month's rent will be due soon after that."

"I know," she said. "By then, I'll have this insurance thing settled. I'll make sure you get paid."

The Friday deadline came and went with no communication from Rachael. Johnny's frustration increased. On Saturday Morning, he dialed Rachael's number and received no answer. After leaving a voice message, he called twice more before dark with the same results.

On Monday, he called again. This time he received a message from *the cellular company that the phone had been disconnected. Johnny was pacing in his office, trying to decide what to do next. He grabbed the mail as soon as it arrived, hoping it would include Rachael's rent check. Instead, mixed in this batch of mail were bills from the electric cooperative and the water department. As he opened them, he noticed they were not final bills. Rachael had not turned the utilities on! Now he was not only stuck without rent but with two utility bills!*

Johnny immediately picked up the phone and called both utility companies and ordered them to turn off the services. Neither could do it before the next day, which was not soon enough for Johnny.

Johnny drove out to the property, hoping to confront Rachael. When he arrived, he banged on the door. Johnny was surprised by the huge man who answered. He was at least 6'4" tall and carried at least 290 pounds on his broad frame. He looked down at Johnny and said, "What do you want?"

"I'm the landlord here to collect the rent," Johnny replied timidly.

"Hang on a minute," the large man said as he closed the door to a crack, turned, and yelled in a gruff voice, "Baby, come to the door!"

When it opened again, Rachael stood there looking disheveled.

"Oh, I'm so sorry," she said as her eyes began to tear up. "We've had all kinds of trouble. After the house burned, our van broke down, and Jimmy got sick."

Johnny had no idea who Jimmy was, but he couldn't resist the tears.

"Okay, please don't cry," he said. "Can you get it to me this week?"

"I'll do the best I can," she promised.

The next day Johnny went to lunch with Dave, a friend who was also a fellow landlord. He told Dave his horror story about the new rental investment.

"What kind of screening did you do?" Dave asked.

"I don't know...she was desperate, her house had just burned down," said Johnny." She was quite nice, and I felt like I could trust her. Then her car broke down and her kid got sick. It just seems like one thing after another."

"You didn't check them out?" Dave asked again.

"I didn't really know how," Johnny confessed.

"Oh, man! You always have to check them out before you let them move in!" Dave said. *"Tell me you at least collected the security deposit before they moved in?"*

"No, I didn't," said Johnny as he tried to hide his embarrassment. *"She had an insurance settlement coming. I felt sorry for her."*

"You need to start an eviction right away," Dave said.

"How do I do that?" Johnny asked.

"Here's the number to my real estate attorney," Dave said, showing the screen of his phone. *"His name is Dan. He'll get you through it."*

"How much will this cost?" Johnny asked.

"It all depends on how long it takes," said Dave. *"Each case can be different."*

6

Since Johnny had already paid a few months' rent out of his pocket, Johnny immediately called Dan and scheduled an appointment with him.

At his first meeting with Dan, Johnny began to learn what an easy mark he had been.

"Did you get an application from them?" Dan asked.

"I have a lease," Johnny said.

"Okay, well, that's a start," he said. "Let me see it."

"Oh yeah, I know this woman," Dan said as he combed through the details. "We evicted her a couple of months ago for ole Bobby Dentweiler. Bobby doesn't ever do screening either. If they can breathe, they can rent one of Bobby's houses. It sure keeps me busy. Did Rachael tell you her house burned?"

"Yes, how did you know?" Johnny asked.

"She said the same thing to Bobby," Dan informed him. "Let me take it from here. But strap in and be ready for the long haul. Rachael and her family are what we like to call professional tenants. They're pros who will go from house to house, looking for a landlord who won't look too closely into their background. They know they can score six months to a year living in your house without paying rent."

"Six months to a year!" Johnny shouted. "How do they get away with that?"

"Well, the eviction process usually takes about two months," said Dan. "But if they know how to work the system, they can stretch that into three months. Most of the time is eaten up by pulling at the landlord's heartstrings as they give excuse after excuse to convince him or her to wait *"just a little longer."*

"So you're telling me she lied about her car breaking down and her kid being sick?" Johnny asked.

"Most likely, yes, and if you give her any more opportunities, she'll do it again," said Dan. *"One more thing I want to prepare you for: the property will probably not be in very good shape when we finally get her out."*

"How much more is this property is going to cost me?" Johnny wondered.

The next two and a half months included four court appearances, a continuance in court, a bankruptcy threat, and three more house payments made without rental income. Finally, the process culminated with Johnny meeting sheriff's deputies at the property and physically moving the tenants' belongings out of the house. Johnny brought along his landlord friend, Dave, and with the deputies' permission, they began slowly moving everything out of the house. By 5 p.m. they were finally finished removing all the contents — every table, every chair, every toy, every piece of clothing, every toiletry — and had changed the locks. When they finished, the house looked like a bomb had detonated in the middle of the living room.

"How do you do this, Dave?" Johnny asked in despair.

"I don't," he said. *"I screen all of my tenants before they move in to prevent this."*

"I guess I have a lot to learn about the rental business," Johnny *conceded.*

Screening is the first chapter of this book simply because it is so important. As a matter of fact, I believe it to be the most critical part of rental property management. Screening out bad tenants on the front end can make your rental house more profitable. And it will also save you a lot of headaches in the long run. Screening for problem tenants is not just about financial issues. You also want to avoid the complainers who are going to call you every time a spider crawls across the floor or each time the neighbor's teenager leaves for school with his car stereo thumping down the road. So, how do you begin?

FIRST CONTACT

Screening begins with the moment of the first contact with the prospective tenant. With the first phone call or email, start asking open-ended questions. If you wind up with short answers to your questions, ask them to elaborate. If they won't, the chances are that they are hiding something. Here are some good examples of questions to aks:

"HOW SOON DO YOU WANT TO MOVE?" This is a great question that may reveal red flags right away. If the prospect says something like "I really need to move this weekend," put on the brakes and find out why. If someone wants to move fast, there is always a reason, and usually it is not good. While there are legitimate reasons that a tenant would want to move quickly — they may have procrastinated and waited until the last minute to find a home, or they might have just found a new job in the area and have to start Monday. That is the nature of some customers.

More often than not, however, someone who needs to move right away is in trouble. It could be their current landlord has begun the eviction process, or they could be hiding from other creditors. In any case, neither way bodes well for your financial relationship with this prospect.

Other prospects may respond to your question about when they are moving with a date in the distant future. It will save you time and money to politely let them know that the home will probably not be available then. They can always check back with you as their moving date approaches. This can be a legitimate answer, too. Perhaps the prospective tenants are students looking to move in for the fall semester of school or transferring into town for a new job. Either way, you most likely do not want to sit on an empty property that long.

"My landlord said I could break the lease," they might say — yet another red flag. I'll definitely want more information on that. Most of the time, this is incorrect — the prospect usually do not even know it — and the landlord will wind up giving them a bad reference for breaking the agreement. To be helpful to the prospect, you may want to let them know the importance of a good landlord reference and suggest they work something out with their current landlord first.

On those rare occasions when the current landlord is willing to allow tenants to break their lease, there is usually a reason, and often not a positive one. They may be slow payers, whiners who complain about everything, or worse, the landlord has actually asked them to move. There are simply not many reasons to let a good tenant out of a lease. A couple of possible examples, however, would be if the landlord wants to sell the house or perhaps to move into the property himself. Be cautious with these explanations because many times, the landlord is just "passing the trash," which will be explained later in this chapter.

"HOW LONG HAVE YOU BEEN LOOKING FOR A HOME?" If the answer is for an extended period of time, they may just be tire kickers. Let them drive by the property before wasting your time.

If their answer to this question is "three months," ask if they have found anything they liked yet or why they haven't found anything. There really isn't any reason to look for a rental home for long periods of time unless your property is in a higher-end or rural market where rentals are rare and specific. It has been my experience that a prospective tenant usually identifies the property they will rent within 72 hours of starting their search.

The next question is loaded and is one of my favorites: "WHY ARE YOU MOVING?" You will get all kinds of answers from this one — from job transfers to "my landlord hates me." This works much better with prospects who are moving locally. If they are moving from North Dakota for a new job, this answer does not tell you anything. It is simply too reasonable. Here you are listening for unreasonable answers such as "my landlord won't kill the snakes in my back yard." Don't let them off the hook with their first response. Continue to probe, asking things like "What else don't you like about your landlord/house/neighborhood?" The more detailed the answer, the more information you will have to make a good decision.

Be polite and helpful. Many times people want what they cannot afford. If you are renting a house for $500 a month, and they complain about the house they are currently renting for $500 a month, chances are they will not be any happier in your home. For example, if they tell you the house they are in is just too old and drafty and their utilities are too high, there is a good chance your house may not be any better at the same rental rate. Unless you can make them understand these economics, you will probably have problems when their first electric bill is due.

Your objective is to get them talking. There are lots of personal questions that you can't ask due to federal fair housing laws. You should brush up on these with qualified legal assistance. But you can glean a lot of useful information with these open-ended questions. The information they offer on their own is fair game.

Also, on the first contact, advise them of your terms. Tell them the monthly rent, the security deposit, and the pet fee, or whether you allow pets, etc. If this does not meet the prospects' needs, and if you are not flexible on your terms, then that is one less time you have to drive out to the property to show it.

You can save yourself time and money on the first contact through careful screening.

APPLICATION

If your prospects pass the first round of questions, the application process begins. Now you need to obtain as much information as possible using a written application. Be very specific with the questions on your application.

A good application should have six basic sections: Resident contact data, income information, residence history, references, signature page, and additional information. It will be a few pages long. If you have multiple roommates applying for one unit (as in student housing), each applicant should fill out their own application.

RESIDENT DATA AND CONTACT INFORMATION: There are a lot of things you need to know about your prospective tenant, not just for screening, but also for tracing them should you need to collect from the individuals after they move out. This data will be sensitive, so be sure you understand the laws regarding handling personal information.

In this section, the least you will need to know is their full name, including middle name if they have one; date of birth; social security number; contact information (cell phone, home phone, email address, etc.); driver's license number and what state of issue; and names of "other residents" who may be children.

INCOME SECTION: The income section is vitally important. I suggest you request the applicant bring a copy of their pay stub to verify that they actually earn what they say they make without contacting the employer. Many employers simply will not provide this information and others will only do it for a fee.

You want the name of their current employer, the employer's location, the length of employment, a work phone number, the position held and in what department, supervisor's name, whether they are full- or part-time employees, and, of course, how much they earn. If they are not employed, you need to know how they earn a living. Ask for other sources of income like social security, disability, retirement, or child support. Make sure you get evidence that these are actually paid to the prospects.

RESIDENCE HISTORY: In the residence history section, go back as far as possible. Ask what the applicant's present address is, how long they were there, the current landlord's name, the landlord's phone number, how much rent they pay, and why they are moving. Then ask about previous residences with the same questions. Repeat this for as many residences as possible. The more information you receive, the better.

REFERENCES: References are especially useful for tracking people down after they have moved out of your property, especially if they owe you rent. This section is more for information you may need in the future than for actual screening. Another good piece of information to collect here is emergency contact information. This data is useful for emergencies (which rarely happen) but even better for post tenancy collections.

ADDITIONAL INFORMATION: This is where you ask the hard questions. For example, "Have you ever filed bankruptcy?" For the most part, I really don't care if a tenant has filed bankruptcy, I want to know if they lie about it (note: if the applicant has recently been discharged from a Chapter 7 Bankruptcy, they typically do not owe any money to anyone, and it is challenging for them to file again anytime soon)

The following is a list of other good questions to ask in this section:

"ARE YOU SUBJECT TO TRANSFER?" If their employment requires them to move around a lot, you may not be able to count on them to be long-term tenants.

"ARE YOU PLANNING ON PURCHASING A HOME?" If they are hooked on the "American Dream" of homeownership (and you suspect they could actually buy a house), this could be a bad sign for a long-term rental agreement. On the other hand, someone who is interested in obtaining a mortgage will have an excellent motivation to maintain a good rental history.

"HAVE YOU EVER BEEN EVICTED FROM A TENANCY OR ASKED TO VACATE?" Evictions will show up on a legal record. But it is more common for tenants to be asked to vacate the rental voluntarily to prevent a long legal battle. When tenants leave on their own, there are often no official records.

"HAVE YOU BEEN CONVICTED FOR ANYTHING OTHER THAN A TRAFFIC VIOLATION?" Notice these questions say "ever." There is no seven or ten-year limit. You want to know if they have "ever," in their entire lives, had a felony conviction.

Note that I have not included a time frame on these questions. I would want the information even if it occurred 20 years ago.

Also, ask what vehicles they will bring to the property. Find out the make, model, year, color, license number, and state of registration.

Ask about pets they plan to have at the home. You need to know how many, breed, weight, age, and color, as well as whether they are housebroken and how long the prospect has owned them.

SIGNATURE PAGE: Finally, you will have your signature page. This is the page that will have a paragraph above the signature line stating what you plan to do with this information. You should also have an authorization on this page that allows you to collect and process this information. You will share this signed authorization with other landlords, property managers, apartment complexes, employers, etc., to let them know that it is okay for them to respond to your request for background information.

Once you have collected this information, charge a fee for processing it if your state allows you to do so. A small fee will eliminate some undesirable tenants. If they are unwilling to pay the cost, it is most likely because they cannot afford it or have something to hide. In either case, you probably do not want them as tenants. By letting prospective tenants know that you are going to check their background, they will understand you will turn them down if they have a questionable history. Often, they will avoid wasting their money by not submitting applications in the first place. This ultimately saves you time, effort, and money.

PROCESSING THE APPLICATION

Now that you have collected all of this information, what do you do with it? Before you begin accepting applications, you should have a system in place. There are specific laws and guidelines that you must follow to process an application. First and foremost is the Fair Credit Reporting Act (FCRA). I cannot go into all the details of the FCRA here — that would be a book unto itself — so I'll hit the highlights.

If you want to process credit information yourself, you have a lot of hoops to jump through and a significant expense. Your place of business must be inspected to ensure that you are following all the rules, such as having locking file cabinets, and that you have a need for the information. Once you get approved, you can use a service to pull the reports needed and see all the financial details on prospects who have authorized you to do so. For most people, that is cost-prohibitive.

If you are able to pull credit reports, don't place too much emphasis on the credit score. Let's face it; most tenants would prefer to own their home rather than rent it. Often, the main reason they do not purchase a home is because of their credit score. One of the largest reasons for a low credit score is due to unpaid medical bills. Unpaid medical bills do not equal a bad tenant. Therefore, most of our customers are going to have less-than-perfect credit, which is the nature of the business. I do not recommend judging someone's creditworthiness based on the incredibly complicated algorithm that goes into producing their credit score. But do look closely at the details in the report. Just because someone owes a hospital $40,000 due to their teenager having an emergency appendectomy does not mean they will be poor tenants.

Abraham Maslow introduced his "Theory of Human Motivation" in 1943, outlining the needs we have as human beings. He concluded that our physiological needs, including housing/shelter, are our highest and most essential needs to fulfill in our lives. While looking into a prospect's background, if you can see that housing (or food, water, sleep, etc.) are not important to them, then something is wrong. It has been my experience that the problem is usually drugs or alcohol abuse, neither of which you want in your rental house. This is why you need to dig deep when looking for property management companies and apartment complexes to which they owe money. Make sure they have been paying their utility bills. If they have outstanding debt on either of these, then housing is not a high priority for them.

Because most landlords, property management companies, and apartment complexes do not report to the credit bureaus, you will need to do a legal search. The legal search is a computer search your screening service should be able to provide you that will show records of lawsuits against the prospect. These are public record, and you can search this yourself. It is very time consuming unless you pay a service to filter the data for you. These services can also help you find information nationwide. What you are looking for are judgments against the applicant from individuals. Many of those will be landlords. The legal search will also show you if an eviction has ever been filed against them in those areas that report to the system you are using.

The final electronic data search is the criminal background check. These are also public record, but there are a lot of records to search through. I recommend using a service to filter these results as well. You will need to determine the threshold at which you are comfortable with a criminal history.

There are services you can use to check landlord references as well, but I prefer to do these myself. I want to hear it from the horse's mouth if I can. The following are a list of questions that I want a current or previous landlord to answer:

- When did the applicant reside at this address?

- How many occupants were there?

- How much was the monthly rent?

- Was the rent-subsidized?

- How many late payments did the applicant have?

- Were utilities included in the rent?

- Did the applicant permit persons other than those on the lease to live in the unit on a regular basis?

- Did the applicant maintain desirable living conditions?

  ◊ If no, please explain.

- Has the applicant damaged any or allowed guests to damage any common areas?

- Has the applicant engaged in any criminal activity, including drug-related crimes in the unit or surrounding area?

- Was the applicant compatible with other residents?

- How was the applicant's overall conduct while residing in the property?

- How was the applicant's supervision and conduct of his or her dependents while on your property?

- Was the applicant's unit in acceptable condition when you last observed it?

- Are you a friend or relative of the applicant?

- Do you have any additional comments?

And the most powerful question of all of them is:

- Would you rent to the applicant in the future?

  ◊ If no, please explain.

The answers to these questions will tell you a lot about the prospects. However, you do have to be careful with landlords who "pass the trash." Passing the trash is an industry term that describes how a landlord will give a tenant a glowing reference to get rid of them. In actuality, they have been terrible tenants, and it is simply easier and more cost-effective to pass them on to the next landlord than to continue to deal with the problem tenants, so they lie on your questionnaire. They don't actually have to lie to pass the trash. Beware of vague answers such as "If qualified" to the question, "Would you rent to the applicant in the future?" One more note on passing the trash: Don't do it! Show professional courtesy to your fellow landlords. Remember, what comes around goes around.

Realize that you won't get all the answers you want. The current landlord obviously cannot tell you the property's condition at move out if the applicants have not left yet. Often too much time has elapsed for useful information. If the tenant occupancy ceased more than three years ago, there is a good chance the records on those prospects have been purged from the system, the unit has been sold, or another management company is now responsible for the home. In these cases, you will not be able to obtain the information you desire, but it is worth the try.

As you go over the results from your electronic searches, be sure to examine the address history the screening service provides carefully. This list will show you where the applicants have received their mail over the past several years. This data can be a red flag if it is very long. Compare this list to the addresses the prospects provided on the application. If you find one or more left off the application, track down the owners of those properties, and ask for references from them.

Some of the missing addresses may be a place of business or their parents' homes, but more often than not, it is a landlord they are trying to hide from you. These are some of the best sources for candid information. These landlords have already "passed the trash" and have no shame against laying it all on the table. Sometimes the prospects may owe them money, and the previous landlord will be glad to find out where they are. If these landlords were intentionally left off an application, it's usually because the prospects know the landlord will provide a poor report.

Once you are satisfied with the paperwork, there is one simple task to complete. This task is one that almost no one does, but is one of the most important screening procedures. It takes a little time and effort, but it is worth it. Climb in your car, program the prospects' current address into your GPS, and let it guide you there. You are trying to learn how they currently live.

This tip has served me well over the years: If your prospective tenants' current home shows little regard for appearance and upkeep, chances are your property will receive similar treatment. When you drive up, you may choose to stop and knock on the door, or maybe you would prefer just to drive by. If the grass is up to your knees and there are toys strewn all over the front yard, you may have learned all you need to know. Sometimes though, it is not that obvious. Look for the tell-tale signs that there may be damage inside. A good indication is the blinds. If they are broken, taped together, or missing altogether, that is a sign of trouble.

I like to stop and knock on the door. Unexpectedly arriving on the applicant's front porch lets the prospect know that you really are doing your due diligence and may even prompt more conversation about their past. Go unannounced, knock on the door with their application in hand, and tell them, "I am processing your application. An inspection of your current home is part of the process. Would you mind if I came in for a moment?" Usually, they will let you in with an explanation that they are in the process of moving, and ask you to excuse the mess. During this inspection, you should be reasonable. Most people do not have their home ready for unexpected guests at any moment. You are looking for damage to the property. Watch for crayon marks on the walls, fist-sized holes in the walls, Kool-Aid stains in the carpet, and the like. Examine the unit for evidence of pests such as cockroaches and fleas. Afterward, politely excuse yourself and tell them that you will get back in touch with them when the report is complete.

The current home inspection accomplishes two goals. The first, obviously, is to determine if they will be a good fit for your house from a lifestyle perspective. Second, and more indirect, it establishes you as a professional landlord. You are putting them on notice that you are serious about your business and intend to protect your home from damage. You are not just going to let them move into your house and forget about them.

After the data is collected, what should you do if you see something you don't like? Turning someone down for a home can be a very tricky process. You cannot rely on instinct alone. You must have an evidential reason to deny them. You must follow the federal, state, and local laws in place. The penalties for violating them can be enormous.

The Federal Fair Housing Act states that you cannot discriminate against anyone from the following seven protected classes:

- Race

- Color

- Religion

- Gender

- Handicap

- Familial Status

- National Origin

You must be careful. It's possible to discriminate against one of these classes without intention. Simply asking prospective tenants if they have children prior to the approval of their application could be considered a violation against the familial status protected class.

As you can see, everyone falls into at least one of the protected classes. Therefore, you must have strict and rigid guidelines for approving or disapproving an applicant. Put these rules in writing and evaluate every applicant with them. Do not break them. Make sure your rules involve only financial and habitability issues. For instance, you may turn down prospects for having an eviction on their record as long as you enforce this rule to every other candidate. As long as none of your rules discriminate against any of the above protected classes, you will have grounds for denial.

Enforcing a rule against having pets, for example, would not discriminate against any of the protected classes. If you apply that rule to an individual who requires a service or companion animal, however, you could violate the Federal Fair Housing Act (handicap protected class).

Fair housing is a very complicated set of laws that actually began with the Civil Rights Act of 1866 and culminated in the Federal Fair Housing Act of 1968, which has been amended twice since then. Most states also have fair housing laws, many of which actually add more protected classes. I can't possibly cover all of this here, so be sure to study the federal and state fair housing laws and consult a qualified attorney if you need advice.

The criminal background check is critical, too. Once again, you have to do this with fair housing rules in mind. It can be seen as discriminatory if you have a "one strike you're out" policy regarding felony convictions (note: arrest records cannot be taken into consideration, only convictions). Have written criteria as to what felony convictions may be acceptable to you and what would not. Assess the entire history of an applicant's background, not just this one item, especially if the offense was decades old. We have to ask ourselves if someone who was convicted of a crime 20 years ago, and has a great history since, does that felony really impact their ability to be a quality resident of your property?

By following rigorous processing procedures, you may learn you are avoiding problem tenants from the start. You will get the reputation in the community that you actually investigate the background of your prospects, and the less desirable tenants will not even bother to turn in an application. It is a waste of time and the application fee for them as well. I've found that less than 10 percent of people who apply for my homes have any criminal record. Usually, those with a criminal record do not even bother to apply.

Every rental property owner would love to require everyone to have a 775 credit score, three good landlord references, and no criminal record. For most of us, however, we would never rent our homes or turn a profit.

Your tolerances will depend on the local rental market of your property and the socio-economic class of your prospects. If your market has very few homes for rent and the demand is high, you can be more restrictive. On the other hand, if your market is depressed, you may have to take a little more risk. Secondly, if you deal primarily with low-income properties, your restrictions will need to be lower as well.

Income is another important criterion that you need to set in your qualifying guidelines. Income ratios are a personal preference, but I cannot imagine anyone renting a property to a prospect who does not produce at least two times the monthly rent. Whatever you select, evaluate everyone identically.

Proving income is not usually an issue. Most companies will let you know if the applicant works for them and how much they make, as long as you have written permission to access this information. Some larger companies may charge a fee to retrieve this information. The easiest way to determine income is to have them produce their pay stubs. However, applicants can always fabricate pay stubs, so that may or may not be enough evidence for you.

Self-employed people pose additional difficulties. Mortgage companies do not like financing self-employed people unless they have been in business for many years. It's best to ask to review their tax returns and 1099's (which can also be fabricated). Unless you really know what you are looking for, however, the information can be hard to decipher. In these cases, your best bet is to contact their work or client references. Find out if your applicants have actually been working for them and for how long. With self-employed people, many times, the best you can get is an estimate.

Many prospects will list "other income" on their application. Most of this is easy to prove. If it is a retirement fund or pension, disability, or social security, they will have a statement to that effect. Child support is another story. Now he or she, and you for that matter, are hoping a third person (the supporting parent) is going to actually pay. Obtain a history of the payments to date. Learn if they have been timely and if they are funded through the court.

If you work in a college town, many students will try to pay with their financial aid. In my opinion, student loans and scholarships are not income. Don't be deceived. It has been my experience that financial aid often dries up just months into a year-long lease.

If the prospects cannot establish enough income, ask for a co-signer. You will prefer a co-signer who is local, but at least one within the state where your property is located. You want someone to collect from if the lessee does not pay the rent or damages the property. Have the co-signer fill out an application and screen them just as you would a tenant, with, maybe, the exception of the drive-by inspection of their current home. If they produce enough income to reach your threshold, then accept the application.

Unfortunately, screening is not foolproof. There are some things for which you cannot screen. You cannot know if someone is going to lose their job after they move in, come down with a devastating disease, file for a divorce, or experience a death in the family. There are a handful of overwhelming family crises that you simply cannot foresee. There is no crystal ball to see into the future.

Furthermore, depending on your screening service provider, only about 70 percent of the nation reports to "the system." Therefore, if someone has committed a felony or been evicted in Smalltown, Tennessee, and Smalltown does not report to the system, you will not know about it. You still want to complete your due diligence to gather all the information you can to mitigate the risk as much as possible. At the very least, you should eliminate the professional tenants.

CONCLUSIONS

So, after reading this chapter you must be asking yourself, "How does all this earn me more money with my rental properties"? It seems like we are spending a lot of our time before we even start. The answer is simple: it can prevent costly problems in the future, not the least of which is an eviction. You will find in this business that turnover is the most expensive element. When you add an eviction to it, it can quickly turn a profit into a loss. We will discuss evictions in more detail in a later chapter.

Another issue you may be able to solve with proper screening is tenant damage to the property. If you can verify that a prospect has a history of damaging property, turn them down and find another candidate. It is simply too expensive to allow someone who does not care about your property to live in your rental unit. Preventing tenant damage by itself can save you thousands of dollars and lots of headaches.

CHAPTER 1 SUMMARY

- Screening is the best way to avoid potential problems and, in turn, ensure more profit on your rental home. It's best to screen for problems before you even have to deal with them.

- Upon the first contact with prospective tenants, ask lots of probing questions. Learn why they are moving, how soon they need a place, and how much they want to spend. Inform them of your qualifying standards, so they can weed themselves out even before you show the property.

- Have the prospects fill out a written application. On the application, ask for additional information regarding their employment, credit history, residence history, and general background. Have a signature page for them to sign informing them of your acceptance criteria and authorizing you to collect the data you need to process the application.

- Don't just say you are going to process an application, actually do it. Run the electronic checks, and dig through the details of their history. Compare the address history you receive to what the prospect gave you. If they are moving locally, drive by the prospects' current residence, and maybe even knock on the door.

- Be sure you understand the Fair Credit Reporting Act and the state and Federal Fair Housing laws.

CHAPTER 2

KEEPING GOOD LONG TERM TENANTS

*D*aniel and Nickie, a newlywed couple married for only four weeks, we're looking for their first home together. After perusing the internet and driving by what seemed to be an endless supply of available homes, they called several potential landlords to schedule viewings of some of those homes for their next day off.

The first one was in a great location. It was near a school they would like their future kids to attend, but the carpet was in deplorable condition, covered in stains, and reeked of animal urine. The next home was in pretty good shape, but the paint was country blue throughout the house and would never match their furniture.

The third house was almost perfect. It wasn't quite close enough to the school they wanted. But they didn't have kids yet anyway so they both decided it didn't really matter. The home was clean with new carpet, fresh neutral paint, some new light fixtures and ceiling fans, and the lawn was lush and well kept. They were very excited to acquire the home.

"We love it," Nickie said to Jack, the landlord, an older man near 70.

"Great, please fill out this application," he said. "I will need you *to pay the application fee before I can process it."*

"No problem," Nickie replied. "How long will it take for us to find out if we can move in?"

"It takes me about a day to get the information I need," Jack answered, as they eagerly filled out the application.

Jack took the young couple's application to his office and began to process it. He ran their credit report and learned that while in college, Daniel had missed a payment to his cellular phone company, but he had paid it off promptly. Otherwise, their credit looked very good. He contacted their previous rental references and landlords, and all the responses were positive. All in all, they looked like a very dependable couple to move into his rental property.

Settling into his chair behind the small desk in his spare bedroom, Jack phoned to let the prospects know the good news. "Hello," he heard a woman's voice answer.

"Good afternoon, Nickie," he said. "This is Jack. I have finished processing your application, and everything turned out fine. When would you like to move in?"

"Oh, that's fantastic!" Said Nickie. "As you know, we are staying with my mom now, so the sooner, the better."

"I'd be happy to meet with you guys this evening after you get off work if you wish," he said.

"That would be great," Nickie replied. "How about 5:30."

"That works great," Jack said. "Remember, you will need to bring

the security deposit and the first month's rent in certified funds with you."

"No problem, I'll stop by the bank on the way there," she said.

Nickie hung up the phone and immediately called Daniel and told him the news. "I love that house, I just can't wait to get moved in," she said.

"Me, too," said Daniel. "I tell you what. I'll bring the camping gear and we'll stay there tonight."

The meeting with Jack that evening went great. They could find nothing wrong with the house on the walkthrough — no stains in the carpet, no plumbing leaks, and no scuffs on the walls. Daniel, Nickie, and Jack signed the lease. As Jack was leaving, Daniel began to bring in the camping gear.

They loved their new home and invited all their friends over for a visit. They couldn't have been happier.

Jack was thrilled as well. As a bit of a control freak with plenty of time on his hands, he frequently drove by the house. It was always clean and the lawn well maintained. To top it all off, Daniel and Nickie paid the rent like clockwork — not even taking advantage of the grace period.

Four months went by, and fall brought cooler temperatures. Finally, one October evening, Daniel decided to turn on the heat. After a couple of hours, he realized the house was not getting warmer. "Should I call Jack?" Daniel asked Nickie.

"No, we can make it until tomorrow morning," she said. "Let's not

bother him tonight."

"Good plan," said Daniel. "I'll just pull out a couple of extra blankets for tonight," Daniel said.

The next morning Daniel called Jack from his office.

"Hey, Jack, we have a little problem," said Daniel. "Our heat never came on last night."

"Oh, I'm sorry to hear that," Jack said. "I'll get over there to take care of it."

That evening, Daniel and Nickie got home and the house was still cold. Nickie was growing frustrated and called Jack and left a message on his answering machine.

The next morning, they still had no heat and the weather forecaster predicted a new cold front was moving in bringing rain. Daniel called Jack again.

"I'll get out there and look at it this morning," Jack promised.

Later in the morning, Jack drove in the cold, blowing rain out to his rental house. He let himself in with his key and tinkered with the thermostat. He soon realized he was incapable of repairing the system, so he called Alton, his heat and air repairman.

Alton showed up 45 minutes later in his rain gear. He opened up the HVAC system acknowledging that it was spotless. It appeared the tenants had been diligent in replacing their filters. Upon further inspection, he noticed a crack in the heat exchanger.

"I'm sorry to say it, but you are going to need a new heat exchanger," Alton told Jack.

"How much is that going to cost?" he asked.

"I'd estimate around $800," Alton said. "But I won't know for sure until I get back to the shop and get pricing."

"$800! That's crazy!" said Jack.

"Come on, Jack, you and I go way back," Alton replied. "You know I wouldn't try to take advantage of you."

"I know, I know," said Jack. "Let me think about it, and I'll call you tomorrow."

Nickie arrived home first that evening and saw where Jack and Alton had left muddy footprints on the floor. She wasn't all that concerned about the mess; she was just thrilled that she would have heat. "Why is the house still cold?" Nickie wondered. She inspected the thermostat, noting its settings were on heat at 70 degrees.

"Crap, still no heat," she thought.

When Daniel arrived, they called Jack and left yet another message on his answering machine. By now they were getting agitated, as they knew tonight was supposed to be the coldest night yet.

Shivering, they huddled under blankets and watched TV for a while before going to bed. When they walked into the master bedroom, their sock feet became wet. As they looked at the floor, they noticed a damp spot on the carpet. Shifting their gaze to the ceiling, they saw a small drip and a growing water stain on the ceiling. Daniel immediately called

Jack, leaving him another irate message.

"That does it!" said Nickie. "We have been without heat now for four days! Tomorrow, I'm looking for another place to live!"

"Why wait until tomorrow?" Daniel asked. "I have my laptop here. Let's see what we can find."

As Jack listened to the two messages from Daniel about how cold it was and about the leak in the roof, Jack thought to himself, "What next?"

Finally, Jack called Alton.

"Okay, go ahead and install the heat exchanger," he said.

"Sure thing, but I'm booked up today," he said. "It seems like everyone's heat went out at the same time. I should be able to take care of it tomorrow afternoon."

Before Jack could dial the phone, it rang. The caller ID identified the call was from Daniel.

"Hello?" he said timidly.

"Jack, we've been without heat now for four days, and now the roof is leaking, "Daniel shouted. "We need this taken care of right away"!

"Daniel, I'm sorry," said Jack. "I just got off the phone with the heat and air company. They said they could take care of it tomorrow."

"Tomorrow isn't soon enough!" Daniel said as he slammed the phone down.

The next day the weather began to clear, but it was still sprinkling off and on. Daniel and Nickie made arrangements to meet at lunch to look at other rental homes. After looking at four of them, they decided on one and filled out the application.

When they arrived home that evening, they found the house toasty warm and were very pleased. They began to reconsider applying for the other rental unit. They called the potential new landlord and removed themselves from consideration.

The roof, however, was still a problem. After dumping a bucket of water collected from the dripping roof leak, they called Jack.

"Thanks so much for taking care of the heat," said Daniel. "It's nice and warm in here. But we have to do something about the roof leak. The stain is getting larger on the ceiling, and we can't keep dumping out buckets."

"As soon as it clears up, I promise I will have a roofer out there," Jack replied.

The next day the weather cleared up enough for Jack to climb on the roof and look it over. The shingles appeared to be in good shape. He couldn't identify a specific problem, so he finally called a roofer.

The roofer informed him that he had a plumbing boot leaking, and it was going to cost $350. Jack explained that he needed to get a second estimate.

Jack left wondering how much more this house was going to cost him and promptly forgot to call another roofer.

Three weeks later, another storm front came through the area.

Once again, the roof began to leak into the master bedroom. Daniel and Nickie didn't even bother calling Jack this time. They simply called the landlord of the house they had applied for three weeks before. He informed them that the home was already taken, so they opened up their laptop and started searching for a new home again.

When they finally called Jack, he explained that he had a roofer take a look at the problem, and he was waiting on a second opinion. This delay further infuriated Daniel and Nickie, who collectively decided that if they survived through the term of their lease, they were definitely not going to renew it.

Jack had the plumbing boot repaired and the roof stopped leaking. However, the large brown stain on the ceiling was a constant reminder of the trouble they had to face just to fix a leaky roof and get heat in the house.

Spring arrived and Daniel and Nickie received a letter from Jack. Jack praised them as excellent tenants and said he would love for them to renew their lease. After reading it, Nickie looked up at Daniel, and they both laughed. They promptly wrote a letter back to Jack, providing him with their formal 30-day notice to move.

Failure to provide excellent customer service is one of the biggest mistakes I see landlords make. There was a day when the owner of a rental house could dictate terms to the tenants. Those days are long gone in most markets. There are simply too many options for residents these days. Landlords must treat their rental property as a business, identify their customers (tenants), and treat them well.

MAINTENANCE

Tenants are much savvier today than they were in the past. Most states, counties, and municipalities have laws governing what maintenance you must do on a residential rental property and what you do not have to do. Most requirements center on essential services and habitability, such as a leak-free roof, dependable electricity, running water, waste removal, and, in many areas, heat and air conditioning. Today, your tenants are aware of this.

I point this out to show that most maintenance to your rental home must be done whether you like it or not. If it has to be done anyway, why not do it in a timely manner? Why wait until your tenant is upset to make the necessary repairs?

Most areas require repairs to essential services to take place within a specified period of time. The rules allow as many as 14 days for the landlord to make the repair. But as you can see from the story above, Daniel and Nickie, who were wonderful tenants, were not going to wait on getting heat in the winter. When it comes to critical services, most won't wait one day, much less 14. It doesn't make sense to wait anyway. If it is something the landlord is required to repair, why not do it today, and keep good tenants happy?

We, as landlords, must think of tenants as customers, not rent checks. For that matter, I have changed the lexicon in my office from "tenant" to "resident" to emphasize their importance to my staff and me. After all, without them, the landlord starves.

Many landlords try to stick their heads in the sand when it comes to maintenance. "Maybe if I ignore it, it will go away" is a common attitude. From time to time, it is as simple as pushing the reset button on a GFCI-(Ground Fault Circuit Interrupter) plug, or maybe the tenant takes care of the maintenance issue for you (usually only when the landlord has not taken care of it promptly) but rarely do maintenance issues just "go away."

Controlling maintenance expenses can be difficult. Things break, and when they do, you must make repairs. The old thought process of "the less I spend, the more I make" is a myth. When you don't spend money on routine maintenance, you simply end up with deferred maintenance costs, drastically reducing the value of your asset and the amount of expected return. The best way to control future maintenance expenses is to repair it right the first time. Correctly fixing maintenance issues sometimes means spending a little more money.

I prefer properties on cruise control — the tenant is happy, paying their rent on time, taking care of the property, and making no maintenance requests. To do this, you need to spend approximately a year's worth of rent every 15 to 25 years on a unit. Remodel the property right, and you won't have to worry about it for a couple of decades. You will still have to deal with turnover and routine maintenance, but you should be able to avoid significant problems.

When tenants call for a maintenance request, thank them. After all, you are the owner of a substantial investment. You want to know when something is wrong. They are helping you preserve that investment. Many times you need to take care of the problem right away to safeguard your property and its value and avoid increased repair expenses. For example, you do not want to let a small drip under a sink persist. The unit can develop mold or suffer rotten floor joists. Most maintenance issues are much less costly if addressed early.

PREVENTIVE MAINTENANCE

There is a lot of disagreement involving preventive maintenance. Many intelligent landlords have conducted cost-benefit analyses that show it is just not profitable. For example, if you send an HVAC technician to service your air conditioning system twice a year at $125 a call, it adds up to $3,750 over the typical life span of an HVAC system of 15 years. You are spending all this to add another few years to a $4,000 system. It really does not make financial sense. Preventive maintenance simply costs too much.

From the standpoint of servicing your customers, however, preventive maintenance can be quite beneficial. Consider HVAC servicing. Frequently, your heat will go out in the coldest part of the year, and the air conditioning will malfunction during the hottest time of the year, the same times that many others experience heat or air conditioning problems. These unpredictable incidents may occur on holidays or weekends when HVAC technician costs are much more expensive. Preventive maintenance can identify issues before they become problems, so your residents rarely have to worry about whether their systems in their house are going to work correctly. Therefore, if you recalculate the cost of preventive maintenance and add the benefit of the intangibles such as lower cost to repair during regular business hours and higher tenant satisfaction, it can be very profitable to do routine preventive maintenance.

CUSTOMER SERVICE

Throughout history, landowners have been the rulers of society, the upper class, the kings. Non-landowners were typically peasants and slaves. To some extent, this attitude persists today. In many markets, the prevailing philosophy has always been, "It's the landlord's way or the highway."

The value of real estate is understood. As the middle class has become wealthier, it has invested much of its wealth in single-family and small multifamily rental homes. With other savvy people investing in similar rental units, we can set ourselves apart by focusing on customer service.

Think about it. You take your car to a shop because you feel the transmission slipping. You come back the next day, pay your bill, and take the car home. You immediately notice the transmission is still slipping. You would probably go back to the shop and question the mechanic as to why it was not repaired correctly. If the mechanic said to you, "If you don't like it, you can go somewhere else," that is precisely what you would do after you raised a little Cain with him, of course — and never return to that shop.

The same situation exists when you lease a home to someone who expects everything to be operational in the house. When they discover it is not, they will confront you, the landlord, to have it repaired, even if it is something simple. If the landlord says, "That's too expensive, take it or leave it," good tenants will probably take the second choice at their first opportunity. This attitude causes turnover, which is one of the more expensive elements of the rental business.

Many landlords lean on the law to avoid doing maintenance to a property. Most local laws are basic when it comes to required maintenance by a landlord, limiting it to essential services and habitability elements, such as electricity, plumbing, a leak-free roof, etc. These essential services may be all the law mandates, but it is not all the market requires. With all the choices a resident has these days, the market will require that you provide more than just a habitable home. It will require that all the appliances work properly, the property is clean and bug-free, etc.

Some may ask, "What choices do tenants really have?" While each market is different, most areas experienced a building boom during the early 2000s. This boom was in all real estate markets — commercial, residential, and multifamily, so there are plenty of choices available. If you are trying to rent a single-family home, you must compete with apartment complexes that offer free Wi-Fi, free cable, swimming pools, workout rooms, and clubhouses. The list goes on and on. Most of these amenities you simply cannot offer. Beyond that, many small investors or large hedge funds have purchased scattered site properties and may be renting the house next door to yours. You are also competing with the home-buying market where residents may buy a home and paint it whatever color they like and have any kind of animal they want. Don't kid yourself. There are a lot of choices out there, especially for the good residents, which are the ones you want.

If you develop a reputation for subpar customer service, residents will not even look at your homes. And if they do rent from you, they may leave at their first opportunity. It is essential to exceed expectations. Provide them pest control. Take care of maintenance requests promptly. Good customer service is soon forgotten, so it must be repeated regularly. On the other hand, bad customer service is rarely forgotten, and forgiveness is hard to come by.

How does one provide good customer service? It begins with open communications. If you are like many landlords, you may feel like no news is good news. You fear to contact the resident because you know they will have something else for you to do. Do not be afraid of that. On the contrary, those situations are opportunities for you to show your excellent customer service. Call, email, or text from time to time just to say hi and ask if everything is okay with the home. When they let you know the sink is dripping, tell them no problem, then have the plumber there by the next day.

Remember that your competition is fierce. Other, sometimes better, available units are why customer service is so important. Develop some fun and inexpensive ideas to keep your good tenants happy. Consider hosting a tenant picnic or an Earth Day celebration, offer a modest discount in December's rent to help offset Christmas expenses, or enter on-time payees into a raffle for a Caribbean cruise. Do something unexpected for them.

There is one caveat to this entire customer service conversation. There is a fine line between customer service and allowing tenants to take advantage of you. I am a firm believer that if I am going to err, I will err on the side of servicing the customer. As you know, maintenance expenses can eat up a lot of profit from your business. Sometimes you identify a resident who is contacting you several times a month, often for trivial matters. You have gone the extra mile, and nothing you do seems to make them happy. Then it is time to teach them the word "no." Sometimes you do have to reset expectations. "No" can result in a turnover as well, but on these occasions, that is often the less expensive option.

BUILD A REPUTATION

It is excellent to take great care of your good residents, but that will do little good if others do not know about it. Build a reputation in your community that you are a professional landlord, not just another slumlord. Building a reputation can be accomplished in several different ways.

First, if your tenants are happy with your service, ask them to let their friends know. In today's day and age of social media, that is relatively easy. Ask them to post a good word on Facebook, Twitter, Instagram, Snapchat, or their preferred social media site. If you have other units available, ask them for referrals for "good residents like them."

It is not just your residents who can spread the word about your properties and your customer-driven approach to business and toot your horn. Establish relationships with local vendors. You need a plumber, electrician, roofer, HVAC technician, and general handyman who will respond to you right away. The best way to do this is to build a reputation for paying your contractors immediately. Some of these contractors are accustomed to waiting up to 30 days to get paid, and sometimes they have to chase checks down, requiring time and effort on their part. They love working for someone they know will take care of them. Then, if you scratch their back, they will be prompt for you when you need service. Once again, ask them to let their friends know how well you take care of your residents.

Finally, celebrate your business relationship with your residents. Invite them to your home, office, or a local park pavilion once or twice a year. Prepare them a good meal and just thank them for sticking with you.

HOW DOES THIS MAKE ME MONEY?

How do good maintenance practices and a customer service focus make you more money in this business? There are three primary reasons: first, you will attract better tenants; second, you will help maintain the value of the investment; and third, and probably most important, you will reduce turnover.

When you rent a well-maintained home, you could have any type of applicants, from excellent to poor. This will allow you to choose the well-qualified tenants and weed out the bad ones, and it will give you the ability to command a higher rent. Poorly maintained property, with doors that do not shut properly, animal urine smells, peeling countertops, or, heaven forbid, pest problems, you will only attract the tenants who either do not care about where they live or cannot otherwise qualify for better housing. Due to the limited market you will attract, you will not be able to earn as much rent as well.

Your investment in a rental property is, most likely, one of the most substantial investments you will ever make. The value of this property will diminish if you do not care for it properly. When a house with deferred maintenance is sold, a buyer must estimate what it will cost to bring the home up to their standard. This estimate will commonly be up to twice the actual cost, decreasing the value of the house. Proper and timely maintenance can prevent many of the things that reduce the value of this considerable investment.

Turnover is one of the most expensive elements of the rental business. When you move one resident out, most likely, you will at least have to touch up the paint, clean the carpet, and polish the unit from top to bottom, while paying expenses you did not have before, such as lawn care, utilities, and trash pickup. You are doing all of this while reaping no income. When you add it all together, a landlord can easily spend or sacrifice two to three months of rent in turnover. Providing excellent customer service can help prevent that situation. You want your good residents to realize what good care you have given when the time to renew the lease comes. The longer you can put off a turnover, the more money you will make.

CHAPTER 2 SUMMARY

- The old days of "the landlord's way or the highway" are gone. If you want to make more money in this business, you must take care of your customers.

- Open communications are vitally important. Be happy to take calls from your residents. Treat those calls as opportunities. Better yet, initiate the contact just to ask how they like their home and how things are going.

- The competition for rental housing today is fierce. Many properties come with freebies. Make sure your rental house is in top-notch condition.

- Perform maintenance in a timely manner. Go above and beyond what your local law requires. Well maintained properties will not only make your customers happy but will help to preserve the value of your investment.

- Build a reputation as a professional landlord in your community. Strive to maintain excellent relationships with not only your residents but also the vendors who you rely on for maintenance and repairs.

CHAPTER 3

PROPERTY CONDITION

*D*onnie Sweat has owned rental houses for most of his life. *He learned the business from his father, who had several himself and left most of them to Donnie when he passed away. Just like his father, Donnie's rental philosophy is, "The less you spend, the more you make." Frequently people would hear him say things such as "If it ain't broke, don't fix it." Lately, Donnie has noticed that his turnover rate has increased and his properties stay empty longer. His rental income seems to be going down instead of up.*

Alice, a prospective tenant, emailed Donnie regarding the ad he placed on Craigslist for his vacant rental home on Main Street. They agreed to meet at 3 p.m. Donnie did not like Alice right off the bat. She criticized everything about the property — the shrubs weren't trimmed, the baseboards weren't clean, the bright blue countertops were ugly.

Lately, Donnie had noticed other prospective tenants making similar complaints. In the past, no one seemed to care about the color of the countertops. He installed them seven years ago because the Habitat for Humanity Re-Store had them available cheap, after some former tenants had damaged the old ones by setting a hot pan on them.

"Why should tenants care what color they are as long as they work?" he would ask himself.

Donnie remembered meeting a man named Tom at an auction a couple of years ago. Tom was a fellow landlord who had different ideas about how to make this business work. Tom had bragged about the top rents he was getting in a matter of days. Donnie still had his card, so he called him and asked if they could meet and talk about how Tom managed his rental properties.

"I'd be happy to," replied Tom. "I'm free after mid-morning tomorrow. Let's meet at one of your empty houses and go to lunch from there."

"Sounds great," said Donnie. "Let's meet around 10:30, and then I'll buy your lunch."

When Tom showed up the next morning, the first thing he noticed was the poor curb appeal. The shrubs were overgrown, the flowerbeds were severely in need of weeding, and the painted front door and porch rails were peeling, generally making the property look undesirable. He got out of the car and shook Donnie's hand as he greeted him:

"Good morning, Mr. Sweat."

"Please, call me Donnie," he replied. "Well, what do you think so far?"

"Let's go inside first," Tom suggested.

Donnie opened the door to a living room covered with threadbare carpet and cloaked in the heavy odor of cigarette smoke. Donnie and Tom stepped inside beneath a ceiling fan that wobbled as it stirred the stale air. Donnie reached over and turned off the switch, shutting down the motor on the fan. It came to a slow stop with a loud clicking sound.

It was then that Donnie and Tom noticed the thick layer of dust on the fan blades.

And it got worse from there. The bright blue countertops glared in the kitchen. The faucet in the kitchen dripped incessantly. There was mildew around the bathtub, and the hallway was dotted with holes where the former tenants had hung pictures.

"Is this house ready for you to rent?" Tom asked.

"Well, I plan to fix the dripping faucet, but what you see is what you get," he said.

The landlords agreed to hold off the discussion about the property until they had ordered lunch, as their chosen restaurant was only a short distance away. During the drive, Tom tried to develop a delicate way of letting Donnie know that his property was unacceptable.

At the restaurant, they took their seats and placed their orders. Donnie pulled out a yellow pad and pen and waited.

Tom looked at Donnie and said, "Exactly how honest do you want me to be?"

"If something doesn't change, I'm going to wind up in the poor house," said Donnie. "I'll take whatever you dish out. I won't hold anything against you."

"In that case, let's start with why I still remembered you after briefly meeting you two years ago," said Tom. "Your reputation precedes you. In rental circles, you are known as 'Mr. Cheap.' People say you are a slumlord who refuses to fix anything."

"That's simply not true!" Donnie exclaimed.

"Now hang on," Tom replied. "You promised you would listen to what I said. I'm just the messenger here. It really doesn't matter if you are a slumlord or not, that's the way you are perceived."

"Okay, I'm sorry," said Donnie. "Please continue."

"The first thing you have to do is begin remodeling some of those properties," Tom said. "I mean top to bottom, side to side. Replace siding, gutters, carpet, paint, and repair or replace anything that does not work properly."

"That would cost a fortune!" Donnie protested.

"Yes, it will," Tom agreed. "You've heard the old saying 'you have to spend money to make money?' That's what you have to do now. I suspect you will spend at least a year's rent on each unit."

"I don't have that kind of money," Donnie said.

"Can you do one of them?" Tom asked.

"Yeah, I guess I could afford that," Donnie said.

"Fine, then remodel the one we walked through today, and see what happens," Tom said. "Frankly, you can't afford not to do this."

"Is that all?" Donnie asked. "Just remodeling?"

"No, you will raise your rent to represent the new value to the property," explained Tom. "You will get more for it, and it will rent faster as well."

After lunch, Donnie thought about Tom's advice on his way home.

He decided that it was time to make these changes. He removed his ad from Craigslist. Then, he called his handyman, Dwayne, and asked him to provide an estimate for updating the house. The remodeling was to include installing new cabinets, countertops, siding, gutters, carpet, and vinyl flooring, and replacing portions of the plumbing and electrical system.

The estimate exceeded the unit's yearly rental income. Donnie dipped into his emergency fund, paid Dwayne a good faith deposit, and signed his contract. Work was to begin immediately.

The work took most of a month, but the result exceeded Donnie's expectations. The curb appeal was much improved and the interior looked like a home he would like to live in himself. He placed his Craigslist ad again with fresh pictures and increased the rental price by $150 a month. Within three days, he had shown it to four different people, including Alice, who still had not found anything. She, along with two other prospects, submitted an application. To Donnie's surprise, Alice's wasn't the best application, so he chose someone else.

"Why didn't I do this a long time ago?" Donnie thought to himself. "Now, I have to figure out which property is next."

Not every property will require the amount of work Donnie completed. But there are usually a handful of things that will improve the quality of most any rental housing. Below we will examine some ideas that may help your financial performance, starting with what type of home to purchase.

WHAT TYPE OF PROPERTY TO PURCHASE

In our opening story, Donnie inherited not only the real estate but also his father's style of doing business. As Donnie demonstrated, the adage "My way or the highway" simply does not work anymore. Unless you are the only game in town, prospective tenants have many choices when it comes to choosing where to spend their rental dollars. Whether you are looking to buy your first or your tenth, rental home, the place to start is at the purchase.

There is no "best" property to purchase. There are better ones than others, but it depends on your investment desires. There are four primary ways to make money in this business: amortization, tax benefits, cash flow, and appreciation. In this section, we will discuss cash flow and appreciation. For the most part, you should get a lot of one or the other. But to get both requires an enormous down payment (or an all-cash purchase) and a lot of luck. Whatever you purchase, you should have at least a little of both.

In my opinion, there is no better income than cash flow. Producing positive cash flow is relatively easy — just put more cash into the project, or better yet, pay for it upfront. Nothing provides cash flows better than a house purchased outright. However, the less money you borrow on the investment, the less value you will receive from amortization and appreciation.

Appreciation is simply the value the property gains over time. During most of American History since the industrial revolution, real estate has appreciated in value. There have been periods and markets, however, where this has not been the case. Some have even suffered depreciation or a reduction in value.

Amortization is an often overlooked method of creating wealth in real estate. With most real estate loans, you pay a little (or a lot depending on how old the loan is) of the loan principal with each payment. This is called amortization. Typically, the principal portion of the payment increases while the interest portion decreases over time. Amortization is what I call "feeding the pig." Each month you are forced to put a little cash into this piggy bank through your payment. As you feed this pig, it gets bigger and bigger, eventually providing you a large feast. Amortization is one way you increase your equity in a property.

Typically, the best cash-on-cash return investments are lower-income houses. You can usually purchase them for a lower amount per square foot and rent them for a higher rate relative to your initial investment. For example, a $100,000 house may rent for $1,000 a month, while a $200,000 house rents for $1,600 a month. The $100K house gets a 1-to-100 ratio monthly while the $200K house only receives a 1-to-125 ratio on the gross return. The more expensive house generates a higher monthly income, but a lower return on investment.

Depending on your market, a good rule of thumb is the house or complex should bring in at least 1 percent of what you pay for the property in expected gross income per month. This guideline will help you eliminate a lot of properties in your search. But it's just the beginning of your data search. From here, you must analyze the expected expenses. Consider things like who pays the utilities, the condition of the units, the amount of taxes, etc.

Low-income properties tend to be maintenance and management

intensive and they typically do not appreciate very well. Let's start with maintenance. You tend to get what you pay for, lower-cost properties are usually cheaper for a reason. Most likely, they are built to building codes (maybe) and that is all. The unit may be older and often will require significant repairs due to deferred maintenance. These factors, along with the simple fact that lower-quality properties generally attract tenants with financial and other problems, cause high turnover rates, and you have a recipe for increased maintenance costs.

Second, lower-income homes are more management intensive. Like I said before, the lower rent often attracts tenants with financial challenges for many different reasons. Your business may suffer from slow payers, evictions, and tenants with drug and alcohol problems. These issues will require you to make more visits to the property and force you to deal with collection issues. If you rely on outside management, it may also result in higher management costs.

Finally, when looking at low-income properties, don't expect them to appreciate much, if at all. You may purchase one of these, bleed cash off of it for ten years, only to sell it for what you gave for it or less. An investor looking to purchase similar properties is just like you, searching for a good cash flow opportunity.

So, who would want to purchase low-income properties? This type of property is perfect for the investor with little upfront cash who likes to be hands-on. Because the income ratio is so much better and the prices are so much lower, the down payment can be small and still provide cash flow. Unless you are managing and maintaining the property yourself, however, that cash flow will not last long. These homes offer an excellent way for a new landlord to get started in this business.

A medium-income property may be more desirable. They are typically located in better neighborhoods and are in better condition. Higher-quality properties attract higher-quality tenants, so you should have less maintenance and management costs. Tenants in these homes are usually more educated and tend to take better care of the property.

Medium-income properties, especially single-family homes, usually appreciate well. Multifamily homes are commonly sold to investors, making the size of the buyers' market very limited. But single-family homes can be opened up to owner-occupants, vastly increasing the number of people who could purchase the property resulting in a potentially higher sales price.

As long as one is caring for the house well, medium-income homes should appreciate with the market at large. Appreciation is one of the most powerful ways to create wealth in our society today, especially when you can leverage it.

Leveraging means to borrow money against an asset. When you leverage a rental home, you have used someone else's money to help pay for the property, in turn increasing your return on the appreciation.

For example, let's say you paid cash for a $100,000 house and that property increased in value at 5 percent in one year. You just earned $5,000 in appreciation on your investment. If you put only 20 percent down and finance the rest, you have still earned $5,000 (appreciation), but now you have only invested $20,000, your down payment. That reflects a 25-percent return on your initial investment. Yes, I have vastly oversimplified this example in an effort to keep you from zoning out with a lot of numbers; this is just to show the incredible power of leverage.

Of course, along with power comes risk. There is almost no risk to owning a house outright, other than opportunity costs. If you do not have a monthly payment, you can almost always rent it and generate positive income or simply sell it. When you leverage property to attempt to get the most bang for your buck, a payment and lien come with it. Now you will be responsible for making that payment regardless of whether your property is rented or not. Furthermore, when you want to sell the property, you will need to get at least the loan amount for the property. Simply stated, be very careful with leverage.

The negative aspects of medium-income properties are cash flow ratios. As stated above, you usually cannot obtain as much cash-on-cash return on an investment that will better appreciate. With relatively less rental income, it makes it harder to cover highly leveraged building payments and all the other expenses that go along with renting homes. The simple cure to this problem is to invest more in the down payment, so monthly payments are more manageable.

What investor prefers medium-income properties? Someone who has adequate money to invest initially will enjoy this type of property, especially if they don't have a lot of time or ability to make repairs to the property. These homes are generally in much better condition, attracting better tenants, and requiring much less maintenance and management. Over time, the property should appreciate more building wealth for the investor.

Finally, there are high-income properties. Each of these homes will have unique issues, so they are harder to generalize. Typically, your cost-to-income ratio will be relatively low, and the purchase will require significant cash reserves.

High-income properties usually attract high-quality tenants. These tenants, however, can be very sophisticated and demanding. Furthermore, they are typically temporary, so the turnover is higher. These types of homes are not ideal properties for the new investor.

THE MAKE READY

Once you have obtained property to rent, you must decide what improvements, if any, must be made to get it ready for tenants. There are different schools of thought here. Many landlords believe the less they spend, the more they make. Decisions are made on cost alone, ignoring the benefits of upgrading the property.

I do not subscribe to this theory. Sometimes you must spend money to make money. Anytime you are considering spending money on your investment, you need to do a cost-benefit analysis. Weigh the pros and cons of your decision. For example, let's say you need to replace a dishwasher. Should you purchase a used one for $50 and install it yourself, or spend $500 for a new one that includes installation. On the surface, it seems the first option is better. After all, a new one is ten times more expensive.

There are several flaws in this line of thinking. First, how long do you expect a used dishwasher to last? You may have to install another one in just a few months. Next is the installation. Yes, an amateur can install a dishwasher, but not efficiently. The amateur may take two or three hours to get the dishwasher functioning properly, while a professional can be in and out in 15 minutes. Consider the landlord's time; it has a high-dollar value. Furthermore, with professional installation, you can generally be assured it will be installed correctly. If problems develop, the installer will return to address any issues. Finally, and by far not the least important point, is the appearance. A used dishwasher is going to look like a used dishwasher. It will be evident to quality prospective tenants that the landlord took the cheap way out and often they will find other housing for their needs. If you add all this up, the used dishwasher may cost much more than a new one.

A good landlord needs to be price-conscious, especially when dealing with low-income housing. But just because a choice is the least expensive doesn't mean it is the best option. These various options are why you need to analyze the costs and benefits associated with each significant expense.

Making the right choice is not always easy. It depends on many different things: your market, type of property, the life expectancy of the product, etc. Let's look at a few different items that may help you along the cost-benefit analysis path.

FLOORING: What type of flooring should you install in your rental house? Most of us would like something hard, cheap, and sturdy... something that will stand up to a lot of abuse. An obvious choice for this would be commercial tiles, like those you would see in a big box store. They are relatively inexpensive and last a long time. The problem with this is they look very institutional and not very inviting. Your market will often dictate the materials you should use. In Florida, there may be high demand for ceramic tile, while in Tennessee, carpet is the order of the day. You need to install the product that appeals to the majority of your prospects.

The type of property you are renting will make a difference as well. In mid- to high-income housing, you may need to install hardwood floors, while in lower-income housing, you may be able to use vinyl flooring. With either choice, you must make sure it is clean and neat, if not new. Improving the condition of the unit will make the property show better, attracting better tenant prospects.

KITCHENS: The quality of the kitchen is highly related to the specific property type. If someone is spending top dollar for a house, they will expect a super sharp kitchen. For the most part, however, the kitchen is a place where the most expensive item may not always be the best choice. For example, granite countertops are beautiful, sturdy, and last a long time, but they are costly, especially compared to a laminate top. A laminate countertop is relatively sturdy and will last for a long time. In the low- to middle-income houses, this should be sufficient.

Kitchens have a lot of components in them. The appearance is important. Everything has to be spotless, floor to ceiling, wall to wall. Also, everything must work properly. There can be no dripping faucets, no knobs missing from the appliances, and it all must operate without any special tricks (such as bumping the dishwasher to get it to start).

PAINT: Everybody has different tastes. Some love flowery wallpaper, while others like stripes. Do not try to keep up with current fads when decorating the house for rent. Keep everything neutral using taupes, grays, or antique whites. Yes, this is a little plain. But your objective is to appeal to the majority of your prospective tenants.

If you have wallpaper or borders, pull them down. These are taste specific and will tend to turn people off. If the paint colors are dark or bright, even in the children's pink or blue bedrooms, get out the paintbrush and cover them with neutral hues.

AMENITIES

The amenities you will need in an appealing rental property will depend on the local market demands and type of housing. There are a lot of decisions to make in this area. Let's address a few possibilities.

APPLIANCES: You may need to provide appliances. For the most part, tenants will not own their cookstove or oven, and very few own a refrigerator. To make your property marketable, you will probably need to supply and guarantee at least those. A dishwasher or built-in microwave, on the other hand, may not be necessary. In very low-income properties, these appliances are probably not expected. But in any middle- or high-income properties, they will be required.

Except in some rare circumstances, I do not recommend providing a clothes washer or dryer. A small majority of tenants may own a washer and dryer, and if they have to store theirs to rent your house, they will find other alternatives. Furthermore, washers and dryers are maintenance headaches. If you do rent a unit with these appliances, try not to guarantee them in your lease (if your market will let you get away with it).

Other devices such as garbage disposals, trash compactors, and smart home equipment will be house and market-specific.

WINDOW SCREENS: In many parts of the country, window screens are imperative, especially in the South, where people love to open their windows. Remember, ultimately, you are trying to sell this home to your prospective tenant, so if the house does not have the amenities they want, they will go somewhere else.

FENCES: Fences can be appealing to prospective tenants, especially if the location is near a busy street or if the prospects have small children. A fence is costly, however, and simply will not pass my cost-benefit analysis. It's great if it is already there, but it would not pay you to install one. Fences are quite attractive to pet owners. If you don't want pets, then you probably don't want a fence.

SWIMMING POOLS: A swimming pool is a nice feature for a tenant, but not so good for the owner of the property. Many tenants don't know how to care for swimming pools, so when the landlord gets the property back, they wind up with a big green mess in the back yard. Increasing liability is a risk as well, swimming pools are considered an "attractive nuisance," which can make the owner of the property liable for an injury or death in a pool. If you have a pool, you will need to check with your insurance company as well. Many insurance companies will require you to provide signage (i.e., "no diving"), fencing, grab poles, and flotation devices around the pool before you can rent the property. Once again, I don't see how a swimming pool can pass a landlord's cost-benefit analysis.

DECKS: A deck brings up images of a summer picnic, outside in the fresh air. Dad is cooking on the grill, mom is serving drinks, and the kids are frolicking barefoot on the warm wood. As attractive as a deck is, they require regular maintenance. If they are not routinely, sealed, and appropriately stained, they begin to warp, rot, and nails start to pop loose. The next thing you know, someone will trip over a warped board or cut their feet on an exposed nail. All things being equal, purchase a home with a concrete patio instead of a deck. If the house already has a deck, budget for a concrete patio replacement when the deck has exceeded its useful life.

STORAGE BUILDING: If your property has a basement, a storage building may not be necessary. If you are doing business in the South where most of the housing is built on a slab or crawl space, however, you may want to provide a small storage building. Unless there is a garage, the tenants will need a place to store things like yard care equipment.

FURNISHED/UNFURNISHED: Whether or not you provide furnishings will depend on your market. Furnished units are popular around military bases and large universities. These are places where there are a lot of young people who have not accumulated the necessities of a household yet. Furnished housing can be very complicated, especially with the inventory. You will need to keep up with every bed, sofa, lamp, etc. Before choosing this route, analyze your market and see what the demand for furnished housing really is and how much more in rent you can expect to get for it.

There are countless other amenities you could provide with rental housing. Each one should enhance the amount of rent you can generate from a unit. Make sure you have done a realistic cost-benefit analysis before deciding to add or remove amenities.

SHOWING THE PROPERTY

Just as you most likely would not buy a car before test driving it, your prospective tenants are going to want to see the interior of the property before they rent it. With few exceptions, you will need to identify an efficient way to show the property.

There are three different ways for a prospect to access a unit: escorted by the landlord or agent, picking up a key, or using a lockbox code.

My preference is to escort a prospect through the property personally. When you or your agent meet the tenant, arrive early, and get the house ready. Make sure the thermostat is set to a reasonable temperature, turn on all the lights, and open all the window dressings and blinds. Lighting up the house will make the property look cleaner (assuming it is clean), brighter, and more substantial. While there, accentuate the positives briefly, and then let the prospects explore the home for themselves. Unless you are asked questions, keep your mouth shut and let them discuss the amenities among themselves.

You don't want to mislead anyone, so you may need to mention any negative aspects. Remember, you will have a relationship with these people for the term of the lease. They will eventually (usually sooner rather than later) find out about the basement that flooded last year.

If you are showing lower-income properties, prospective tenants will often complain about the condition of the home. Emphasize the economic value of the house. They need to understand that in real estate, as with most of life, you get what you pay for.

Always be conscious of safety when you meet prospects to show them the property. You never know who you will be meeting, so make sure you have easy access to something like pepper spray and let someone know where you are going and when you are expected to return.

You can also allow prospects to access the property by picking up a key at your office. Ask for a small deposit — maybe $20 — to ensure they return the key. You can refund the deposit when they return the key.

Finally, if you use lockboxes, you can provide the prospect a code to the box to access the key. A lockbox is a small combination key safe that hangs on a doorknob or a wall. The combination is usually three or four digits, so they are easy to remember. Most people today have easy access to a phone that has a digital camera. Have the prospect take a picture of their photo ID and send it to you electronically before you give them the code to the lockbox. Having them provide you photo identification could help prevent abuse of the lockbox system.

The problem with the last two methods is there is no protection for the rental unit. Someone could take the key and make copies or just move in if they wanted. You also can not protect the property from potential damage, either intentional, such as graffiti, or unintentional, such as muddy footprints on the new carpet.

None of these methods are wrong. Use whatever process works best for you in your market and circumstances.

One more thing on showings. Beware of renting something sight unseen. Many parts of the country are growing rapidly and you may encounter situations where someone is moving in from out of state and can't visit the property before signing the lease or giving the holding deposit. With modern technology, there are lots of ways to address this situation. Pictures and videos of units can be viewed electronically. But you can't smell a house or get a feel for the neighborhood, or hear everyday noises over the internet. Many times I have had people move into a house sight unseen, even after a family member looked at for them, only for the new tenant to hate the home. Then you are stuck with upset tenants for the term of the lease.

How does any of this increase the revenue of your rental property? Ensuring that your property is in top condition will attract more tenants to your home, expanding your pool of possible tenants, and ultimately increasing the amount of rent you can command. More revenue is the direct result of higher-quality properties. Tenants will be happier and more willing to remain in the unit after their lease is over, decreasing turnover.

CHAPTER 3 SUMMARY

- Low-income rental properties can increase your cash flow, but also intensify management problems and increase maintenance expenses.

- Regardless of what type of property you rent, the house must be clean with fresh paint and all components in working order before you lease it to a new tenant.

- Higher-quality properties attract higher-quality tenants and yield higher rents. Better condition homes produce better applicants and higher rental income.

- Required amenities are determined by the competitive properties in your market area. Ensure that all amenities function correctly.

- There are three methods of showing a property, owner/agent escorted, picking up a key from your office or home, and providing a prospect a code to a lockbox to enter the property themselves. Use whatever method works for your situation.

CHAPTER 4

MOVE-OUTS AND COLLECTIONS

*B*obby and Sarah bought their third rental house last month. They had so much good fortune with the other two that they could not wait to close on this last one. So far, everything had gone smoothly. They had managed rental properties for three years and had never had to evict anyone or deal with a deadbeat tenant. Their rental income had been flowing on time with minimal maintenance. Their cash flow was almost 20 percent more than they forecasted when they bought their first rental property.

They were excited about another rental home purchase, and they anticipated getting a new quality tenant. Bobby placed an ad on Craigslist for their home for rent. It was a typical "for rent" ad, featuring a three-bedroom, two-bath home available on the north side of town. It was near two schools and rent was $1,200 a month. Bobby felt that the monthly rent might be a little high, but thought it was worth a try. He could always come down.

They received a few phone inquiries and scheduled a couple of showings, none of which yielded an application.

"Maybe we should reduce the rent amount," Sarah said to Bobby at dinner one evening.

"If I haven't rented it by this weekend, we'll drop it to $1,150," said Bobby.

Sarah agreed, and they finished their meal.

Later that evening, the phone rang. Bobby nor Sarah recognized the number on the caller ID, so they assumed it was a prospective tenant. Sarah answered the phone.

After a brief greeting, Sarah said to the caller: "Like it says on Craigslist, it's a three-bedroom, two-bath house for $1,200 a month... yes, it has a chain-link fence around the back yard, but the garage has been converted into a den...I don't know. Let me check."

"Can you show the house tomorrow afternoon?" Sarah said to Booby as she covered the phone's mouthpiece with her hand.

"I could go by there at lunch," Bobby replied. "Otherwise, it would have to be after work."

"Let me check with her," Sarah said, motioning to the phone.

After exchanging a few more words, Sarah hung up with the prospective tenant. "She's going to meet you at noon," she said to Bobby.

"Great, what was her name?" Bobby asked.

"I can't remember," said Sarah. "It was Teri or Mary or something."

The next day, Bobby arrived at the house just before noon. He was on his lunch break from his day job, so he was a bit rushed. Bobby opened the door, turned on all the lights, and opened all the mini blinds. He noticed a spider building a new home in the corner of the living room, so he retrieved a rag from his truck and wiped it away.

The prospect arrived in a blue Chevy Nova. She climbed out of the car, closing the door behind her and introduced herself.

"Hello, my name is Teri Phillips," she said. "I spoke to your wife on the phone yesterday."

"Hello, Teri," Bobby said, extending his hand to shake hers. "It's nice to meet you. Come on in, and take a look. It's a great location — walking distance from both the elementary and middle school."

"Yes, that was one of the things I liked about the house," she said.

"Just let me know if you have any questions," Bobby said as she toured the house.

After a few minutes, Teri returned and asked, "When will it be available?"

"I could have it ready for you today," Bobby replied. "When did you need it?"

"The sooner, the better," she said. "I would love to get my kids in those schools."

"Great," said Bobby. "Let me get you an application."

Bobby was looking at his watch, waiting for Teri to fill out the application, knowing he was going to be late getting back to work, but he felt like this was more important, especially if he could get $1,200 a month. He would make up some excuse for being late if he needed to.

Finally, Teri finished filling out the paperwork and said, "here it is," as she handed the completed application back to him.

"Thanks so much. I'll work on this today and get back with you as soon as possible," Bobby said, rushing her out the door.

"Good. I look forward to hearing from you."

On his way back to his office, Bobby texted Sarah, informing her of the application he had received. Sarah was an elementary school teacher, so he did not expect her to reply quickly, but she did texting *"Awesome! Will she agree to $1,200?*

At the next stoplight, he texted, *"Yes."*

He arrived at his office, frustrated by his tardiness. Fortunately, it appeared no one noticed but him. Later that day, he began processing the application. His electronic investigation came back just okay at best. Teri's credit score was very low, and she had several past-due accounts. But when he called the landlord references on her application, both said she had been a stellar tenant.

That night Sarah and Bobby reviewed the application. They were both concerned about the credit score and past-due balance, but the landlord references set Bobby's mind at ease.

"Who were they?" Sarah asked.

"I don't know, the people on her application," said Bobby.

"Can we trust them?" Said Sarah.

"Come on, she was really nice and wanted to get her kids in those schools," said Bobby. *"And she is willing to pay the $1,200 a month,"*

"Okay, let's go for it," Sarah reluctantly agreed.

Bobby called Teri to give her the good news and offer the house to her. Teri seemed excited when she heard the news.

"Can I move in tonight?" she asked.

"Well, I would prefer tomorrow," Bobby said. "That will give me the chance to pick up anything I've left behind and my "for rent" sign. How about tomorrow, mid-day?"

"Okay, noon again?" Teri asked.

"Sure," said Bobby. "Remember, I will need the first month's rent and a security deposit of $1,000. I will have all the paperwork ready."

"$1,000! I didn't know it would be that much," said Teri. "Can I bring you half of it and pay the rest in $100 installments over the next five months?"

The alarm bells went off in the back of Bobby's mind, but he felt pressured after he had already offered her the unit.

"I suppose that will be okay," he reluctantly replied.

"Great! See you tomorrow at noon," Teri said as she hung up.

The next morning Bobby had the lease paperwork ready and took it with him. Once again, he left his office at 11:45 to make sure he would be there on time. He knew this appointment would take him a little longer, so he told his boss he would be late coming back from lunch.

"You were late yesterday, too," said Jack, his boss. "Is everything okay?"

So much for nobody noticing.

"Yes, everything is just fine," Bobby explained. "I am meeting a tenant at my rental house to have them sign a lease."

"Oh, I understand," said Jack. "I have a few rental homes as well. Take all the time you need. Just don't make a habit of it."

Bobby arrived at the house and gathered his sign and a couple of small items Sarah and he had left behind when they cleaned the house. He heard Teri pull into the driveway.

Bobby met her at the front door and invited her in. They walked into the kitchen, and he gave her the condition check sheet and told her to walk through the house and note any damage that she didn't want to be held responsible for when she moved out.

Teri took her time walking through the house. Finally, she returned to the kitchen, signed the check sheet, and handed it to Bobby, who also signed it. Bobby then pulled out the lease, and they went over all eight pages.

"Do you have any questions?" Bobby asked as he finished.

"No," said Teri.

"Then just sign at the bottom," Bobby said. Teri did so, and then Bobby added his signature.

Teri handed Bobby a personal check for the first month's rent and half of the security deposit.

"I know I agreed only to take half the security deposit upfront, but

I want you to know this is not the way I normally do business," he said. "At the first sign of trouble, I will take the necessary action to move you out if necessary."

"I understand and I appreciate your trust in me," said Teri. "You know how it is when school starts. It costs an arm and a leg. I will probably have the remaining security deposit paid off long before it's due."

"Okay," said Bobby as he handed her the keys.

As he was driving back to his office, he thought to himself how sweet Teri was and how much he liked her. Still, something just didn't feel right.

After work, Bobby went by the bank and deposited Teri's check in the night deposit box.

Five months passed, and Teri indeed kept her promise to pay the remaining security deposit and had made her rent payments promptly. Bobby began to relax. Then came month six. It was the middle of winter, and the rent due date came and went with no check from Teri.

Bobby called Teri to check on her.

"Hey, Teri, is everything okay?" He asked.

"I'm so sorry, Bobby," Teri replied. "I have lost my job. I hoped to have another one by the time the rent was due, but it has been very hard."

Now Bobby had a sinking feeling in the pit of his stomach.

"So, what is your plan?" He said.

"I don't know," said Teri. "I am trying really hard to find a job. In the meantime, my unemployment will kick in next week."

"Unemployment only pays a fraction of what you were earning," Bobby said. "How are you going to pay the rent on that?"

"I'll figure it out, I promise," said Teri.

"Okay, but I must have the rent by the end of the week," Bobby said.

"I'll get it to you somehow," Teri replied and hung up the phone.

It was the seventh of the month, and Bobby and Sarah had already collected from all of their other rental homes, all of which were due on the first. They were becoming very concerned about Teri.

At the end of the week, they still had received no payment or communications from Teri.

"One of us has to call her," Sarah said to Bobby, who heard "you have to call her."

"Gosh, I hate this," he replied as he picked up the phone.

Bobby dialed Teri's number. There was one ring and then an automated message informed him that the number was no longer in service.

Bobby hung up, looked at Sarah.

"Her phone has been disconnected," he said.

"Then one of us is going to have to go over there," Sarah said, and Bobby understood as "You have to go over there."

Bobby reluctantly agreed.

"I'll go with you," Sarah said.

They drove in frustrated silence to the rental house they were once so happy to purchase, both thinking what a pain it had become. When they arrived, they noticed the grass hadn't been cut in a good while, the shrubs were not trimmed, and toys were strewn all over the lawn.

"Maybe she has moved," Bobby said hopefully.

Bobby got out of the car, while Sarah stayed behind. Knocking on the door, Bobby noticed an offensive odor he could not identify. A child of about four years old opened the door. Bobby said, "Hello, is your mom at home?"

"Mommy," the little boy yelled.

A short, overweight woman wearing an old dirty t-shirt and compression shorts showed up at the door.

"I'm the landlord, and I'm here for the rent," Bobby said to the woman he didn't recognize.

"Teri's not here," she said. "I think she's looking for a job."

"Who are you?" Bobby asked.

"I'm her sister," she said. "I'm just here for a little while watching the kids while she's out."

"Would you let her know I stopped by and tell her to call me,

please?" said Bobby.

"Sure," Teri's sister said.

As Bobby climbed back into the car, Sarah asked, "Who was that?"

"She said she was Teri's sister," said Bobby. "She is babysitting while Teri is looking for work."

"What do you think?" Sarah said.

"I think we're in big trouble," Bobby confessed. "The house smelled awful; the mini-blinds were torn and, from what I could see, the inside was filthy."

"So what should we do," she asked.

"Let's give her a couple more days and see what happens," said Bobby.

The next week, they still had not heard from Teri. When Bobby tried to call her, the number remained disconnected. He drove to the rental house on his way home from work. He noticed the same odor when he knocked on the door. Teri's sister peaked through the mini-blinds covering the window to the left of the door, then disappeared inside. After a couple of awkward minutes, Teri finally came to the door.

"I have to get the rent," Bobby said. "I need to make my house payment."

"I'm so sorry," said Teri, almost in tears. "I'm trying really hard, but I just can't find a job. My unemployment just isn't enough after I get food. I even had my phone shut off."

"Yes, I noticed," said Bobby. "Do you have another number where I can reach you?"

"Not yet," she said.

"Teri, this isn't working," said Bobby. "You either need to move by the end of this weekend or pay the rent."

"I really don't want to move, so I'll do what I can to get the rent," she said.

"What about your sister?" Bobby asked. "Can she help with the rent?"

"Oh no, she is on disability," Teri explained. "It's just enough to feed her kids."

Bobby wanted to address the condition of the house, but he decided it would be best to cross one bridge at a time and concentrate on collecting the rent.

"I expect you to either turn your keys in or pay the rent by Monday morning," Bobby demanded.

"Okay," Teri replied as tears began to run down her cheek.

Bobby stepped off the stoop and headed home. On his way home, he began to wonder what an eviction would cost.

The next morning at work, Bobby approached Jack and asked, "How much does an eviction cost?"

"It's not so much the cost as it is the time," explained Jack. "It will take two to three months from the time you start. How far behind are *they?"*

"How did you know I had a tenant that was behind?" Bobby said.

"I didn't figure you would ask the question otherwise," Jack replied.

"It's the new rental," said Bobby. "They are already a month and a half behind."

"You don't want to let them get that far behind," Jack cautioned. "Let me get you my real estate attorney's number. He can get you started."

"She said she would either pay or be out by Monday," Bobby said.

"Do you really believe that?" Jack asked.

"Now that you ask, I guess not," Bobby admitted.

"Start the eviction today," said Jack. "The longer you wait to begin, the longer it takes."

"How much will he charge?" Bobby asked.

"About $400 in attorney's fees and another $125 in court costs," said Jack. "It could be more, depending on how many times he has to go to court."

"Wow, I didn't know it would cost that much," said Bobby.

Bobby and Sarah discussed it that evening and decided to see if Teri would come through on Monday before they spent the money on an eviction.

Monday evening arrived, and there still had been no communication from Teri. Bobby drove over to the rental house and knocked on the door.

"I'm sorry, Bobby," Teri said. "I just don't have it."

"But you agreed to move or have the rent by today," Bobby said.

"I don't have anywhere to go," said Teri. "Besides, my kids are enrolled in these schools."

"You are leaving me no choice," Bobby said.

"I don't know what to tell you," Teri said. "I'm sure I'll get a job soon."

Bobby left the rental home, determined to begin the eviction. He called Jack's attorney the next morning from his office. They agreed to meet at the attorney's office during Bobby's lunch break.

Bobby walked the seven blocks to the attorney's office. A heavyset man in a suit reached his hand out and introduced himself.

"I'm Pat," he said. "Nice to meet you."

"My name is Bobby," he replied. "It's nice to meet you."

"Tell me the problem," said Pat.

Bobby went through the story from the beginning. The entire time Pat was shaking his head.

"If I have done the math right, she is almost two months behind on you now," he said.

"Yes sir," said Bobby. "That's about right."

"I wish you had come to see me six weeks ago," the lawyer said.

"I'll get it started for you. I will need a check for $525 to start. That will include your court costs, paperwork, and up to two trips to court for you. I bill by the hour after that, and if we have to get a writ of possession, you will need to pay for that."

"What is a writ of possession?" Bobby asked.

"That's the document from the court that gives us the authority to remove the belongings from the property," Pat explained. "It cost $85 payable to the court."

"Ouch, this could get very expensive," Bobby said.

"That is not the worst of it," Pat said. "If we have to go through the entire eviction, the process will take about 60 days to complete. During that time, there will be no rent coming in for you".

"How much worse can this get?" Bobby asked rhetorically.

"I'll do what I can to make it as painless as possible," Pat said.

That night, Bobby told Sarah about the conversation with Pat. Sarah was distraught, but they were both thankful that they had an emergency fund. They declared this an emergency, cashed a check, and continued to make their payments.

The two court dates and fifty-nine days went by very slowly. Finally, they had to purchase the writ of possession.

"It's up to you now," Pat said as he handed Bobby the writ.

"What do you mean?" Bobby asked. "What do I do now?"

"Now you remove the belongings from the house," Pat said.

"Me,"! Bobby exclaimed.

"Yes, you," said Pat. "No one else is going to do it. Call this number and make an appointment with the sheriff's department. They will meet you out there, but only to keep the peace. They are not going to pick up anything, unless it is a weapon or an illegal object, such as drug paraphernalia".

Bobby and Sarah took the day off work to meet the deputies on the scheduled day. They hired a couple of laborers and met them all at the house at 10 a.m. The deputies knocked on the door, escorted the occupants out of the house, and told Bobby and Sarah to get started.

Bobby, Sarah, and the two laborers spent the day moving the beds, clothes, toys, TV's, sofa's, tables, etc., to the street, while Teri and her kids watched. Upon finishing, Bobby changed the locks and went home.

That weekend, he went back to the house to clean up. There was still stuff in the front yard that Bobby had to haul away. He was appalled at the condition of the house. After all the work he and Sarah had put into it before Teri moved in, they were now going to have to paint and clean for the next two weeks' worth of evenings and weekends.

He cornered Jack at the office on Monday morning.

"What did I do wrong?" Asked Bobby.

"It looks like you did a decent job of screening, but you may have been a little greedy on the rent amount," said Jack. "There are some things you just can't predict. Job loss is one of those things. If you don't have a realistic expectation of collecting rent in a timely manner, move fast on the eviction proceedings. Don't wait!"

Dealing with tenant turnover is never easy, especially when the tenant doesn't want to go. Managing rental properties is a people business. When you are dealing with people, something can (and often will) go wrong, no matter how good a job you do. Many times hard decisions have to be made. When making tough decisions, it is essential not to procrastinate. In this chapter, we will discuss the art of collections and the move-out.

NORMAL COLLECTION PROCEDURES

There are many different ways to collect your weekly or monthly rents. But most important is to create a procedure and stick to it.

First, check your local and state laws. Many specify grace periods that you must honor before you can take any action. For example, if your rent is due on the first, but the state requires a five-day grace period, you will not be able to charge a late fee or begin an eviction until after that fifth day. Furthermore, many states require that the last day be a business day. Therefore, if the fifth of the month falls on a Sunday or a federal holiday, you must wait until the end of business of the next business day to take any action.

Set up your rent collection policies in a way that works best for your business. To get you started, I'll give you an example that we use in our office. Rent is due on the first and is considered late after the fifth of each month. On the sixth of each month, late fees are charged to the tenants who have failed to pay. From the sixth to the 10th of each month, the tenant will receive repeated polite communications (phone calls, text, email, etc.) informing them in a considerate manner that we have not received the rent. Our objective here is to open communications, without which nothing gets done.

From the 10th to the 15th of each month, the interactions with the tenant will become more firm — pay up or get out. The 15th is what I call "drop dead day." That does not mean that I send them to the legal office at that point. It means that I evaluate the realistic possibility of collecting the rent.

Let's face it, an eviction is expensive and should be avoided when possible. You do not want to make a hasty decision to evict a tenant, but you don't want to procrastinate either. The longer you wait to begin, the longer the process takes. If you have a realistic expectation of collecting the rent in a reasonable period of time, hold off on sending the file to a legal office. If not, file for the eviction.

What is a "realistic expectation?" That could be a lot of things. Here are a few examples:

The tenant has been excellent in the past and has a legitimate and temporary bad situation and has given a written promise to pay the rent by a date in the near future;

The tenant has documented evidence (i.e., Payroll slip, a letter from a church or other benevolent agency) that the funds are on the way;

An otherwise good tenant is traveling and on their way home.

As you can see, all of these require communication. If the tenant has ignored your calls and messages, you don't have a choice but to move forward with the eviction process.

Other landlords hold to another school of thought on when to begin an eviction. Many believe that giving a break only wastes time. Therefore, after the grace period expires, they will start the eviction process right away. If you choose this approach, you establish yourself as a landlord who will not tolerate late payments. I completely understand this reasoning and endorse it. Choose whatever works best for your business.

One more thing on late rent, I highly recommend that you do not take a personal check for rent paid after your grace period ends. Depending on the bank you use and the bank on which the check is drawn, it can take up to two weeks to learn that a check is bad. If you accept the check late and it bounces, it will delay the eviction process. Let your tenants know up front that any late payments must be in the form of a money order or cashier's check. Furthermore, if a tenant ever writes you a bad check, require all future rent to be paid in certified funds.

I know landlords who prefer to take cash. I disagree, especially if you have a large number of units. First, you do not want to be known as a person who carries a large amount of cash on the same date every month. That invites trouble from robbers or muggers.

Second, cash has no paper trail. There is no evidence of whether or not payment has been made. If a tenant writes a check or electronically pays you from their bank, there will be a paper trail for that payment. If you do not take cash payments, they can't come to you and say they paid you in cash. Furthermore, sometimes we landlords make mistakes, miscount a payment, or occasionally lose one. A cleared check provides the tenant evidence showing their made payment. On the other hand, a check that doesn't clear their account can reflect a lost payment and can be easily rectified.

Third, I do not recommend playing games with the Internal Revenue Service. If you have earned the income, pay your fair share to the government. In an audit, they will discover it anyway. And there are severe penalties for cheating, including jail time. It is simply not worth the risk.

Money orders are an acceptable option for tenants who do not have checking accounts. As long as tenants are filling them out properly, they are safer to carry than cash. If they are made payable to you, you are the only one who can cash it. If you ever have trouble with a money order, however, it can take months to settle the problem, depending on the company that issued the money order. For the tenant, a money order can offer proof of payment, assuming they retain the stubs from the money order. Retaining this documentation requires some good record-keeping on behalf of the tenants.

Electronic payments are another excellent way to collect rent. Automated Clearing House (ACH) payments are much like electronic checks. Money flows directly from the tenants' checking or savings account into your bank account, with no paper but an excellent electronic record. Keep in mind, ACH payments can bounce just like a check, but notification of a bounced ACH payment happens more quickly.

You can also accept credit card payments for rent, but they are more expensive than other methods. You will pay a small percentage to the credit card company for each transaction. These small percentages can add up quickly when we are talking about a sizeable monthly expense like rent. And many credit cards offer the consumer (tenant) the opportunity to challenge a payment for up to six months after making their payment. When this happens, the credit card company can electronically remove the money from your account. You will have to weigh the risks and determine if the convenience is worth the risk for your business.

LATE FEES

Some landlords believe higher late fees do more to deter late payments. Their philosophy is to charge as much as they can, and as often as possible. Once again, it is advisable to check your local and state laws. Most of them have a cap on how much you can charge for all different kinds of fees.

Earning top dollar on your rental property doesn't necessarily mean charging as much as you can. As you have seen from earlier chapters, charging more than a property is worth can actually lose you money. The same goes for late fees.

A late fee is only good for the landlord if it is collectible. Let's say the state will allow you to collect up to 10 percent in late fees, so you charge the maximum amount. If a tenant is already struggling to pay the base rent, adding so much in late fees just puts them further behind. As time goes on, after only paying the rent and not including the late fees, they get further and further behind. Before you know it, you are evicting tenants who are only behind because of the heavy late fee burden. In this situation, nobody wins, not the tenant or the landlord.

I suggest you make your late fee collectible. You want to encourage your tenants to pay on time, so it has to hurt a little, but not so much that they cannot pay it. How much to charge in late fees depends on your market. If you are renting low-income properties, your late fee should be minimal, $15 to $25. If you are renting homes in the $1,000.00 a month range, charge around $50.00. A good guideline is 5 percent of the rental amount.

HARD DECISIONS

Ultimately, if you stay in this business long enough, hard decisions will have to be made. You will finally get a tenant who does not pay their rent, sneaks in a roommate or pet, trashes the house, or otherwise breaches the lease agreement. At this point, the best advice is, don't wait. Make the decision and proceed.

When you have determined that the tenancy should not continue, begin by negotiating with the tenant. Allow them to move on their own accord. Typically, they know they are behind and cannot catch up. Many of them will jump at the chance to get out without an eviction on their record.

If the offer of letting them leave without an eviction does not work, you may want to try an approach commonly called "cash for keys." Offer the tenant some money, maybe a few hundred dollars, if they turn in the keys to you by a specific date. I know this goes against the landlord grain, but often it is less expensive than an eviction. Remember, making money is what this is all about. Sometimes you have to spend money to make (or save) money.

If all else fails, then file for the eviction. The eviction process varies vastly from state to state, so it is difficult to give an example of how the process works for all 50 states. Each state, county, and municipality will have a process that you need to learn and understand, preferably before getting into this business. Consult a trusted attorney or judge in your area to learn about the process. When I say local, I mean the city in which the property is located. The process can change from city to city. Depending on your state and whether your paperwork is in order, it could take two weeks to six months to forcibly remove a tenant from your property. Worse yet, if you did not conduct appropriate screening and got a professional tenant who understands the system, it could take even longer.

Do not ignore your state and local laws. Most states have very stiff penalties (some including jail time) for forcibly removing a tenant without going through the proper judicial process. Furthermore, there are stiff penalties for "constructive evictions." Constructive eviction is when the landlord does something to the property to make it uninhabitable, such as disconnecting the utilities, removing doors or windows, or disabling the heat and air system.

POST TENANCY COLLECTIONS

Once tenants have left the property, either by their own choice or by force, it is challenging to collect any monies owed to the landlord. I have seen many statistics on this, most showing that there is approximately a 6 percent collection rate, post tenancy. The limited ability to collect past due monies after a tenant has moved is one of the largest reasons you do not want to be too hasty when forcing someone out of a house. If you think you can collect the rent, be patient...but not too patient.

If you are good at it, you will have the most success working on collecting back rent yourself. It is a matter of diligence and perseverance to continue to locate and contact the former tenants. If you choose to work on past tenant collections yourself, become very familiar with the Fair Debt Collections Act. There are rules you must comply with to proceed.

Most of us are not very good at constantly reminding former tenants they owe us money, especially after they are gone and hard to find. Landlords have already moved on to other more profitable endeavors, such as finding a new tenant for the vacant unit. It's better to let the professionals conduct post-tenancy collections for you. Find a reputable collection agency, negotiate a fee with them (many will only charge you a percentage of what they collect), and let them take over.

You can use garnishments, but only if you have a legal judgment against the former tenant. To get a garnishment, you will have to take them to court and get the judge/jury to agree with you that they owe you the money. Anytime you have to sue somebody, it is a long, time consuming, and costly process. Therefore, you must determine if the past tenant is "judgment proof." A judgment-proof tenant is one who has little or no income, few assets, and little or no prospects of having either income or assets. It has been my experience that pretty much covers almost all of the tenants that have moved away owing me money. Nine times out of 10, you are better off forgetting it and moving on, than spending time, effort, and money to sue them.

One more thing you can do is either join the credit bureau or hire a collection agency that is a member of the credit bureau. Many times you can place back rent and damages on a credit report. If the tenants get their act together and ultimately have income and assets and try to purchase a car or house, your collection will be there waiting. Most likely, they will not be able to close on that house without paying you first.

CHAPTER 4 SUMMARY

- Establish clear procedures for collecting rents and make sure the tenant is aware of them before move-in.

- Do not take cash. Cash can be dangerous and offers no evidence of payment for the lessor or lessee.

- Make your late fees collectible, so they do not drag an otherwise good tenant into eviction.

- Landlording is a people business, and things will go wrong. When making hard decisions, make them quickly.

- Evictions are a painful, expensive, and time-consuming process. Avoid them if at all possible, but if you must resort to eviction, don't hesitate.

- The average post-tenancy collection rate is 6 percent. Hire a good collection agency to help you with these collections.

CHAPTER 5

———— · ● · ● · ————

GETTING TOP RENTS

J *im owns a duplex and noticed the unit next door was to be auctioned on Thursday afternoon. Knowing his friend, Robert, was in the market for a rental property, he called him to let him know. Later that day, they both met at Jim's duplex, so they could walk around and see the property for sale next door.*

"It looks like it is in good shape," Jim said to Robert.

"Maybe even better than yours," Robert replied, knowing he was right. The one for sale appeared to have no deferred maintenance — the windows were in good shape, the roof looked only a few years old, and the driveways gravel was recently spread. They decided to attend the auction.

Robert set out to learn all he could about the property, He examined the tax records and deed, where he learned the owner had recently died, and the sale was part of her estate. The tax notices had been mailed to the duplex, indicating that the owner had lived there. He could not find any history regarding the rental rates the property had produced in the past, so he called Jim to ask how much rent he was receiving for his duplex next door.

"They're both two-bedroom units," Jim said. "The right side rents

for $550, and the left side rents for $575. The only problem I have had is that it sometimes takes a little time to rent when it turns over."

"That's good information," Robert replied. "Thanks."

Robert was excited when he and Jim arrived at the property on the day of the auction. He had every intention of buying the property if he could get it for around $100,000. The auctioneer opened the doors to both units, and Jim and Robert walked through. The inside of the home was cared for as well as the outside with new carpet, fresh paint, and a recent cleaning.

Stepping back outside, he noticed a crowd beginning to form. Robert sized up the competition, writing off several of them as merely nosy neighbors. But there were at least three other men who appeared to be real bidders. He wondered what they would cost him in the end.

The auctioneer opened the sale with his standard disclosure speech, explaining that he didn't know anything about the building and whoever bought it was taking it as-is/where-is with no guarantees. After properly covering his liability, the auctioneer began the bidding at $50,000. Robert quickly chimed in, and the race was on. Within five minutes, the bid rose to $90,000 with offers from all of the men Robert expected to be real bidders.

The auction stalled at $90,000 for several minutes, and the auctioneer tried to milk Robert for a higher bid, staring at him and flashing a huge toothy grin, while nodding and flailing his hands. He kept pressuring Robert just to bid another $500. Finally, Robert caved and nodded his head. The auctioneer jerked around, tossed his right hand in the air, and yelled something incomprehensible that sounded *somewhat like a high-pitched frog in the woods. The auctioneer lost interest in Robert and devoted his attention to the other men who had been bidding. One bidder was pacing back and forth, unable to commit, while the other had dialed his phone to consult with someone at the other end. The auctioneer then took a break from his illegible calling.*

Several minutes later, the bidder with the phone shook his head and walked away. Now all the attention was on the pacing bidder, who quickened his nervous strut. Robert could envision the numbers circling his head, as he finally gave up. Waving off the auctioneer, the pacing bidder sat down.

Finally, the auctioneer began the count down.

"$90,500, going once," he announced, pausing for effect. "$90,500, going twice…" when he was suddenly interrupted by a dramatic burst from one of his ring men, who screamed, "$91,000!"

Feeling like a child who just had his ice cream cone ripped from his hand, Robert turned to see who had outbid him. To his surprise, it was one of the nosy neighbors. They proceeded to bid against each other for the next several minutes, with Robert finally offering $101,000 while saying to himself that was all he would do. Once again, the auctioneer began the count down. Just before the final gavel fell, Robert looked at the other bidder, who tipped his hat to him as the auctioneer yelled, "Gone!"

With a little case of buyer's remorse, Robert looked at Jim and said, "What do you think?"

Jim reassured him that his decision was sound, so Robert signed the papers.

The next day Robert began his plan to rent the property. As far as he could tell, there was nothing he needed to do to the building or yard to improve his prospects. It was already in top-notch condition. He researched the market and determined that $550 to $575 a month was indeed the market price for each unit. He had 30 days before he closed on the duplex, however, so he decided to shoot for the moon. He placed an ad on Craigslist for a "two-bedroom duplex in excellent condition available for $699 a month."

After receiving no inquiries for four days, Robert decided to adjust his pricing a bit. With the better part of the month to go before closing on the duplex, he still kept the price higher than he expected to get. Robert dropped the amount in his ad to $675 a month and decided to drive by the property. Pleased with the clean appearance of the building and excited about his purchase, he looked next door at Jim's duplex and noticed one of the front doors standing open and junk strewn across the front yard. Robert picked up his phone to call Jim and let him know.

"Hey Jim, I'm out here at the duplex now, and it looks like someone has moved out of one side of yours," Robert reported.

"I was kind of expecting that," said Jim. "The tenants in Unit A had gotten behind on their rent, so I told them to pay up or get out. I guess they chose to get out."

"Meet me at Starbucks, and we'll get some coffee," said Robert. "Then I'll go walk through it with you."

"That'd be great!" said Jim. "I'll see you there in about 10 *minutes."*

After purchasing one caramel macchiato and one white chocolate mocha, they left Robert's car in the Starbucks parking lot and drove over to the duplexes in Jim's truck.

"I appreciate you going with me," said Jim. "You never know what to expect when doing a walk through after someone skips on you in the middle of the night. It's nice to have company."

"No problem," said Robert. "I know how it is."

"Have you started marketing yours yet?" asked Jim.

"Yes, I priced it at $699 a few days ago with no response, so I lowered it to $675 this morning," he replied.

"Whew! $675 seems a little high, don't you think?" said Jim. "The best I've ever been able to get was $575."

"Maybe, but I have some time before I even start paying for the duplex," said Robert. "I might as well try to get more while it doesn't cost me anything."

As they pulled into the driveway at Jim's duplex, it was hard for him to hide his frustration. White plastic bags, broken flower pots, discarded newspapers, and faded toys were strewn across the front yard. As they entered the open front door, they were greeted by the odor of animal urine and stale cigarette smoke. The tenants had taken all the furniture, but they had left behind broken electronics, opened food items, trash, and dozens of clothes hangers. Two tread-bare automobile tires, several empty gas cans, and a crippled lawnmower had been abandoned in the back yard along with more trash piled on the carport.

"Here we go again," Jim said.

"Does this happen often?" asked Robert.

"More often than I would like," he admitted. "I'll get it cleaned up, and rent it again."

"I guess you'll have to replace that carpet," Robert said. "It smells awful."

"No, I'll have Harry clean it," Jim said.

Jim and his crew spent the next week cleaning and touching up the paint on his duplex. Knowing that Robert had advertised his unit at $650, he decided to increase the rent for his unit to $600 a month.

With a little more than a week left before he closed on the property, Robert began to see some activity on his available rental. After receiving three requests to view the property, he called the auctioneer to make sure it was okay to show it.

"Sure, that's no problem, but I recommend that you don't sign any leases until after you close," he advised. "Anything can happen to stall or terminate a real estate deal."

Robert scheduled appointments for three interested parties for the following Saturday morning.

"$650 seems like a lot for your two-bedroom unit," said the first gentleman after his walkthrough. "I can get the one next door for $600."

"I understand that," Robert said. "The owner of that house is a

friend of mine, so if that is more attractive to you, by all means, take it before someone else does."

After walking through the unit again, the prospect who complained about the price filled out an application, paid an application fee, and left Robert with a security deposit to hold the unit.

"We saw your friend's property, and it doesn't compare to yours," he said. *"You can't blame a guy for trying to get a better deal."*

"I sure can't," said Robert. *"I'll process your application Monday morning and get back to you."*

The other two prospects took applications with them and went on their way.

Robert met Jim later that afternoon and shared his excitement about the strong prospect.

"That's incredible," Jim said, *"At least a dozen people walked through mine, and no one has shown any interest, even for $50 less than yours."*

"Interesting," Robert replied.

The remaining weekend's worth of advertising yielded several more inquiries about Robert's duplex and another appointment to see it on Monday afternoon. Monday was just as successful as Saturday. A couple who had just looked at Jim's unit walked over to Robert and said, *"Can we take a look?"*

"Sure," Robert said. *"Just let me know if you have any questions."*

Five minutes later, the prospects said, "We'll take it."

Again, Robert went home with an application, application fee, and a security deposit.

Both applicants turned out to have reasonable credit scores, no criminal history, and excellent landlord references. Robert promptly accepted both applications and terminated his advertising.

In the meantime, Jim was tired of having his unit sit empty, so he finally reduced his price to $575. This price was still more than he had gotten in the past. He showed the unit over and over, but with no takers.

Robert closed on the duplex and moved his new tenants in two days later.

"I don't understand," Jim said to Robert. "My unit is the same as yours, and you are getting $100 more with better tenants. What's up with that?"

"It's all about the condition of the property," Robert said. "If you rent higher-quality units, you will attract higher-quality tenants, and be able to turn away those you don't want in your house."

"I can see that, but I don't have the money to do what they did to your duplex," said Jim.

"In that case, you will collect less rent and have to settle for less desirable tenants," Robert said.

Realizing that time (especially vacancy time) is money, Jim reduced his advertised rent to $550 and finally accepted $525 from a less-than-stellar tenant two weeks later.

Tired of the ongoing struggle, he asked Robert for advice.

"Start saving now, and plan to put about a year's worth of rent into the building," Robert said. "Replace the windows, cabinets, appliances, and flooring and address all of the deferred maintenance. Then, put the property on the market as I did. Place your advertisement at a higher price than you think it will bring. Make small adjustments every few days until you get the activity you want."

Realizing that Robert would collect an extra $2,400 a year, and have a duplex that was practically maintenance and trouble-free, Jim sighed.

"I agree," he said. "That's exactly what I'm going to do."

There are five things, and only five things that make a property rent: location, timing, condition, terms, and price. In this chapter, we will look at each of these and a few other items to help you get top rental income for your property promptly.

LOCATION

If you have ever studied real estate, you know that the three most important things to remember are location, location, and location. I agree that where the property is located its most crucial attribute. Because the location is so important, I have listed it first. But to be clear, location alone never has and will never cause a piece of property to be rented. The market is so large and so complex that it cannot be determined by just one item.

I discussed the best type of property to purchase in Chapter 3. It's essential to research your local market to determine what configuration of a home is renting best. It's also vital to research the best locations in that market. Almost every market will have different segments for the various socioeconomic classes. The upper-income neighborhoods will be on one side of town, while the low-income areas will be on "the other side of the tracks." You need to determine which areas are the best for rental property.

Most of the time, upper-income neighborhoods are not the best places for profitable rental homes. Residents in those areas are more likely to own their homes than to rent. Furthermore, you receive a smaller financial return on properties with more square footage. Allow me to explain. Prospective tenants tend to inquire about the number of bedrooms and bathrooms and whether the property has a garage. They rarely ask about square footage. Therefore, a three-bedroom, two bath-house that is 2,000 square feet will rent for only about 10 to 20 percent more than a three-bedroom, two-bath home with only 1,300 square feet. Based on the square footage, you will pay approximately 35 percent more for the larger house and only receive 10 to 20 percent more rent. (There are some exceptions to this application. For example, the expense of the square footage for basements or bonus rooms over the garage is very inexpensive additions during construction.) Therefore, financially speaking, most of us would avoid higher-income, single-family homes when choosing rental properties.

Because there are readily available customers (tenants), middle-income rental units usually offer more stable tenants and a better appreciation of the property over time. They are also more easily sold if you need to liquidate relatively fast since many middle-income people are homeowners as well. Typically, you will require less maintenance on these homes, which can save a lot of money in the long run.

Lower-income units tend to generate increased rental income relative to square footage and initial investment. They usually have a better cash return, but appreciate very little. They are more management intensive and typically require more maintenance, so these homes are perfect for the "hands-on" investor who wants to handle the tenants and repairs themselves instead of hiring it out.

Location goes beyond the "good" and "bad" parts of town. Your market will show you where to look. It may be close to bus or subway stops, near factories or office complexes, or adjacent to a preferred school district. However, beware of chasing school zones, it has been my experience that zones change frequently, and a "good" school may lose its appeal when a "better" school opens across town. Talk with key people in your area to help determine where to purchase the right property.

TIMING

Of all five items that make a property rent, timing is probably the least important and the least controllable. You simply cannot know in advance when the market will change. With that being said, there are naturally better times than others to rent a house. If you are in the Northeast, Midwest, Northwest, or Canada, it can be challenging to entice people to move when they must deal with heavy snow and frigid temperatures.

On the other hand, a typically good time to get top dollar in rents is in late July and August, just before the kids go back to school, especially if you have a university in your market. Late spring tends to be another appealing time to rent a property, as people are getting over the deep winter freeze. In some markets, the week between Christmas and New Year's is a good time for people to move. Not only do people have the time to do it then, but many corporate leases also want to begin at the start of the company's fiscal year.

Don't fool yourself into thinking you can time the market. Before the great recession (2008-2012), rents tended to increase by a relatively small percentage year after year. It was easy to predict how much rent you could expect in the future and plan for it. During the great recession, the real estate market was walloped. (Some have referred to it as a "real estate depression.") Home values plummeted and rents typically dropped 30 percent across the board (some markets saw more than a 60 percent decrease). Dropping property values and rents had a tremendous effect on our market. Rental rates now fluctuate, sometimes very quickly. One month they will be up, while the next they will be down. You can learn the market value of your property by testing the market, which we will discuss in the pricing section of this chapter.

CONDITION

We discussed the value of the condition of rental property in detail in Chapter 3, so I won't beat a dead horse here. Suffice it to say; if you want top dollar on a vacant property, it must be in top-notch condition. It must have a fresh coat of paint, clean baseboards, spotless carpet, sparkling appliances, dust-free ceiling fans, trimmed shrubs, scrubbed tubs and toilets, and a freshly mowed lawn, among other things.

A unit that is clean and well cared for will attract a better quality tenant. You would not want to rent to a resident who keeps a sloppy house, so do not show them one. Showing property in good shape will help you to be selective in your choice of tenants.

The good condition should not only translate into a higher monthly rent but also increase the rentability of the property. A unit in top-notch condition will rent faster than one dire need of attention. This translates to a quicker occupancy equaling more money in the landlord's pocket.

I simply cannot stress enough the importance of excellence in the condition of your rental properties. Even low-income units must be in great shape. Once again, it comes down to the quality of the tenant. Just because someone is in the lower socioeconomic class does not mean that they will automatically be bad tenants. If you offer them poor units, however, you will attract the poor performing residents.

TERMS

"Terms" are all the little things that you will require of your tenants other than the monthly rent. Terms may or may not be in the lease. Some examples of terms that can affect your rental price are the security deposit, cleaning fees, and your policies on pets and smoking.

SECURITY DEPOSIT: A security deposit is there for the protection of the landlord. In the event something goes wrong with the business relationship, the landlord may be able to use it to pay for any damages to the property. If the terms and conditions of the lease have been completed with no problems, however, a security deposit is entirely refundable.

CLEANING FEES: A cleaning fee is an up-front charge to a tenant to pay for getting the property ready for another tenant when the lease is up. It is important to understand the semantics when drawing up a lease. By definition, a deposit is refundable; a fee is not. There is no such thing as a non-refundable deposit.

To protect yourself, you should attempt to get as much money as you can (or that the law will allow in your area) up-front. The amount will be dictated, once again, by the market. If you are trying to collect three times the rent in a security deposit, while the rest of the market is only asking for half a month's rent, your unit will be rejected. You must be reasonable when asking for a deposit, while at the same time protecting yourself as much as you can.

PETS: Allowing pets can cost you a lot of money and earn you a lot of money at the same time. The American Pet Products Association (APPA) says that 68 percent of American households are pet owners (The 2017-2018 APPA National Pet Owners Survey Debut, AmericanPetProducts.org). So, if you say "no pets" in your unit, you are automatically eliminating 68 percent of your tenant pool. If you are renting single-family homes or units with a yard, that elimination number could be as high as 75 percent, since non-pet owners are more likely to live in a condominium, townhouse, or apartment. This high percentage of pet ownership is a fundamental shift in the landlording business. In the past, we could get away with not taking pets. You still can, however, it will cost you.

A smaller tenant pool translates to lower rental rates and longer vacancy periods, both of which cost a landlord a lot of income. I suggest you try to capitalize on the pet craze by charging the tenant fees for their beloved pets. Pet fees can be an up-front, one-time charge, or a monthly pet rent as long as the pet is at the property. Evaluate your market to determine which will be more profitable for you and acceptable to your renters.

I know that pets can (and do) cause damage to rental homes, which is simply a cost of doing business. Besides, I estimate that once you add up the pet rent lost, longer vacancy period, and lower rent collected, it may cost you as much as $200 a month to not allow pets. If your average tenancy period is two years (another added benefit of taking pets is that tenancy periods are usually longer), that is $4,800 more that a landlord earns. It would be unusual that a pet would do enough damage to cost more than $4,800, plus the security deposit you are holding.

Once again, compare these statistics to your local market. A more transient market, such as one around a military base, may boast a decreased incidence of pet ownership, while a more rural market may have a higher rate.

SMOKING: Cigarette smoking is much less socially acceptable than it has been in the past. Therefore, we see fewer and fewer smokers. From a landlord's perspective, this is a good thing. Cigarette smoke gets into everything — drapes, carpet, paint, drywall, and even concrete.

Your local market, as well as the properties you decide to own, will dictate whether you allow smoking or not. Typically, tenants from the lower socioeconomic class are more likely to be tobacco users. They will be more likely to rent than more affluent people. Therefore, if you are renting lower-income properties, you may have to accept that your tenants will smoke in your units.

If you ban smoking, you will often eliminate such a large percentage of your market that you will have to accept lower rents, extend your vacancy periods, and the tenants may just lie to you and smoke in the house anyway.

Dozens of other terms can be included in your relationship with the tenant. Many of these can be profit centers. Some landlords will offer lawn care or cleaning services and others may include the utilities paid with their rent. Do what works in your area.

PRICE

Pricing your rental home right is another critical aspect of marketing your property. In today's world, 83 percent of people looking for a home used the internet as a search tool, according to the National Association of Realtors (Real Estate in a Digital Age 2017 Report, NAR.Realtor). Being online, stacked up with all the other available rental units, means that your property has become commoditized. The prospects can go from one house to the next simply with the click of a button. They can compare photos and features of prospective homes. The first question will usually be the preferred price (followed by the number of bedrooms and bathrooms). Many of the popular websites allow prospects to specify details of the property they are seeking: number of bedrooms, number of baths, garage size, etc. The first question will usually be the preferred price. Therefore, if you overprice your unit, your ad will never appear on the prospect's screen.

Owners of property do not determine the price of their rental home. The market does. The market dictates all the financial aspects of this business. If you rely on multiple web sites and other advertising means to market your property, and you still do not receive any responses, then the market is rejecting your pricing. It is time to adjust your price.

If you are unsure of how to price your property, try testing the market. Research the price of similar properties to determine what your unit should bring. Search the same web sites you expect prospective tenants to use and see where other landlords are pricing their units. Remember, these are only asking prices that the market may be rejecting, too, but it is a place to start.

After determining an estimated rent amount, and if you can afford to let your property stand vacant for a little while, add about 10 percent to that number and start your marketing there. Most of the time, you will know very quickly if you have hit the target. My experience has been there is only an average of 72 hours between the time prospects decide to find a new home and the time they identify the property they will rent. It can be a swift process. If, after five days or so, you have not received any clicks on your internet ads, no requests for showings, and no applications, you haven't found the market price. Make a small reduction. If the property should rent for less than $1,000 a month, decrease your rent in $25 increments (if rent is more than $1,000 a month, adjust the price in $50 increments), and try again. Adjust the price every five days or so, until you begin to see the activity that indicates interest in the property. Once there, stop and see if the responses continue.

The above process is what I call "Testing the Market." Testing the market is one of the best approaches to earn the most money in the landlording business. As you already know, vacancy costs money, so it is vitally important that you do not waste time with this. Make your price adjustments promptly. Do not wait any more than seven days if you have found that the market has rejected your price. Every day that property is empty, your vacancy cost goes up. It is simply not worth waiting around for two months to collect another $50 on a one-year lease when you could have had it rented in two days for $50 less. Do the math. You will see what I mean.

One caveat to testing the market: timing can affect the results. If you have a property become available at a poor time in your area (such as winter in the northern states and Canada, just after school starts in a college town, or a general market crash), that may skew your results. You will receive poor results due to the market being small or even nonexistent. In this case, you may be better off taking less for the property, or offering a shorter-term lease, so you can then market the property at a better time.

Once again, do the math to determine what is better financially. Do what you can to get a property filled promptly. One of the worst things you can do to a home is leaving it empty. When a house is empty, humidity begins to loosen glues throughout the house, or the cold freezes it. Things start to leak and no one is there to observe and report it. Squatters or animals could move in, forcing you to remove them. Even during the bad times, do what you have to do to fill the properties.

During the great recession, many of us just could not figure out what was going on. Vacancy rates around the country reached record highs, and properties stayed on the market for months. It just didn't make sense. After all, if people could not buy houses, they would have to rent, correct? As landlords, we pulled out all the stops, offered move in's with the first month's rent free, printed signage that read "Pets

Welcome," and gave away cruises to anyone who rented a unit. Nothing seemed to work.

In hindsight, we can see what happened. Those millions of Americans who were dealing with foreclosures or bankruptcies could not qualify for rental housing either, leaving them with no choice but to move in with relatives or friends. The job market was so miserable for college graduates that many chose to move back in with their parents. The bottom line was America stopped creating households. At the same time, many of those foreclosures were snapped up by investors who, in turn, placed them on the rental market.

It was merely a supply-and-demand problem, economics 101. There was too much supply and not enough demand. The only thing that was going to get those units rented was a lower price. The rental amount had to keep dropping until it found demand from those who could afford it. Chasing the price down was the ultimate exercise in testing the market.

Since then, rents have bounced up and down. No more of this steady, predictable growth rate. Rent can be up one month and down the next. Testing the market is more important today, even for the experienced landlord, than ever.

NEGOTIATING

Although the five items I listed above are the only things that will influence your ability to rent a property, there are other things you can do to increase the revenue from your rental property. I will be dedicating the rest of this chapter to these.

First, be prepared to negotiate. It may be in your best interest to dicker with prospective tenants. If rentals are filling quickly, you may have multiple applications at once on a unit. In this case, let all the prospects know that you have other interested parties, and open up a sealed-bid process. Give them a few hours to get back with you with their highest and best offer to rent the home. Note, I said, "highest and best." The highest is not always best. You may prefer a tenant with no pets or who does not smoke and be willing to take a little less rent in those circumstances.

The sealed bid process can scare all the prospects off, however, and then you are forced to start your marketing process over. I encourage you only to attempt this when properties are turning over very quickly. If there is a lot of inventory available, the prospects will simply find another home.

If your market is slow, you may want to negotiate a longer-term on the lease. As we have discussed earlier, turnover is the most expensive aspect of the rental business. If tenants are willing to sign a longer lease, it may be in your best interest to take less rent in return.

It may sound counterintuitive, but sometimes you can make more by taking less. Sometimes finding well-qualified applicants can be very difficult. When you find those tenants, be prepared to take a little less in rent with the anticipation that it will cost you less in the future. Prospects who require less management, are less needy, and are likely to follow through with their lease provisions and leave the property in excellent condition, can save you a lot of money and headaches. Be reasonable. Do not offer a 25-percent discount, but consider a 5-percent reduction. It is a nice reward for prospects with excellent history.

Be ready for market shifts. They can come without notice and happen very quickly. When you are testing your market price, do not stop on the price reductions until you hit the market. The temptation is to stop at the amount your last tenant was paying. If the market has changed (or if the condition is not as good or if the timing is off), it may not be worth that much anymore. Waiting months to fill a unit can cost thousands of dollars compared to taking a $50 reduction on the rental rate. Fill the unit now for what you can get for it.

Market shifts can happen for any number of reasons, from macroeconomic, like the great recession of the late 2000s that affected the entire country, to local issues, like school zoning changes or more desirable developments on the other side of town. Whatever the reason, be ready for it.

As a lease comes to an end, negotiating begins again. If the market has improved, you may want to increase the rent. Beware, a rent increase may cause a turnover. If you have good tenants, the risk of vacancy is often not worth a small increase in the rent. On the other hand, if the market has dropped, you may want to institute a "good-tenant discount" for a lease renewal. If they have been good tenants and you would like to retain them, give them a reason to stay. Many times a small decrease in the rent will prevent them from looking at the open market and moving.

MARKETING

You may have all the items in line for the market — the right price, excellent condition, perfect location, reasonable terms, and great timing — but none of this matters if you do not tell anyone your property is available. Marketing could be a book unto itself, so we are just going to hit the high points in this chapter. Here are some ideas to let people know that your awesome unit is ready to rent.

INTERNET: It is vitally important that you advertise your homes online, and on multiple websites. Dozens of websites can provide you with an online presence, including many that are free! Be careful, however, as there are a lot of scam artists online who prey on those who are not well versed in internet scams. Before making any deals with prospects, verify their identity at the very least and never offer any private or banking information.

PRINT MEDIA: Newspapers, magazines, and ad booklets are examples of print media. These forms of advertising are becoming less and less effective as the internet continues to grow. The internet has become our society's preferred outlet for information. However, some demographics may still rely on print. If you are renting a property in an over-55 community or senior housing, ad circulars (the small slick paper magazines you may see at local restaurants) may be your best choice. Also, lower-income people are less likely to be connected to the internet, so they may search for housing using the newspaper. In this case, the paper may be a good outlet for you. When I do my cost-benefit analysis, I usually find that, in general, print media does not offer a good return on my investment.

SIGNAGE: Do not overlook the power of yard signs. Some of your best inquiries will come from signs. When prospects call you from a yard sign, they already know the neighborhood, have noticed the curb appeal of the house, and usually have a general idea of how much it should cost per month. Typically, they have already pre-qualified themselves and know whether they can afford the property. Keep in mind, the sign you use represents your business. If you use an old sign picked up at the local hardware store, held together by duct tape, with the price or phone number marked through, and reprinted with a felt marker, this will scream that you are a cheap landlord. I recommend having your sign (or signs) professionally produced by a local sign company. They will cost a little more, but they will last longer and show your professionalism. When they get old and worn out, throw them away and get new ones. Nothing ruins the otherwise excellent curb appeal of a rental home more quickly than a cheap or run-down sign. One last thing on signs, a sign can indicate a property is empty. If your area has problems with squatters or vandalism, you may not want to use them.

SOCIAL MEDIA: In today's world, if you want to get information out to a lot of people, there is nothing more powerful than social media. Sites like Facebook, Linkedin, Twitter, Instagram, and others can pass on information to thousands (maybe even millions) of people with a click of a button or a tap on a screen. When you have a unit coming available, let your connections know on whatever social media sites you use. If you do not use social media, start. There will be a small learning curve, but it is not too difficult for anyone. Remember not to abuse social media. Your friends and acquaintances do not want you inundating them with ads for your rental home, but every now and then will not hurt.

FLYERS: The simple advertising flyer can be an inexpensive, but effective, form of advertising. If you are using a service to produce your internet ads, you may be able to print a flyer from that ad. Be sure to print them in color. As with signs, the brochure represents you, and you do not want to appear cheap. Post the flyer on community boards. You can find these boards in many local businesses and government facilities, such as grocery stores, restaurants, local housing agencies, etc. If the unit is near a university or college campus, there will be many boards where you can advertise your vacancy.

TELEVISION/RADIO: Unless you are renting dozens of properties, television and radio will probably be cost-prohibitive. You might reach out to your local media outlets, however, to see about advertising in the classified section of their websites. As with everything, evaluate the cost-benefit analysis before you buy it.

OTHER FEES

Income generated from a rental property does not have to be limited to rent. There are plenty of other income sources you may want to consider. Here are a few for you to consider.

APPLICATION FEES: Charge the prospect an up-front, non-refundable fee to process an application. After all, it is a lot of work to run the reports, call employers, communicate with previous landlords, and finally, drive by the applicant's current home. You should be compensated for these efforts. Charging an application fee works exceptionally well in a good market. In a less robust market, however, you do not want to discourage a prospect from filling out an application. Some states will only allow you to charge what it actually costs you to process an app, and it cannot be a profit center, so be sure to be aware of your state laws.

LATE FEES: On most leases, there is a date when the rent is due each month. A late fee is a penalty to the tenant for paying their rent beyond that point. Late fees are not just "free money," they cover the cost of the landlord's collection efforts. Be cautious as to how much you charge. You want to charge enough for the price of paying the rent late to sting, but if you impose too much, it may not be collectible. The last thing you want is to file for eviction over unpaid late fees. Check your state laws as many states limit the amount a landlord can charge for late fees.

PET FEES/PET RENT: With so many prospective tenants owning pets, take advantage of it. Charge them for the privilege. It can be a one-time upfront fee or an added amount to the monthly rent. We determined that pets are a part of life in the rental business. Why not make a little money on it? I encourage you not to take a pet "deposit." A deposit, by definition, is refundable, and in most states, a pet deposit can only be kept by the landlord for pet damage. In that case, the tenants could burn the building down, and if you could not show any pet damage, you would have to return their pet deposit.

COIN OPERATED MACHINES: If your building is large enough, you could add a coin-operated laundry area or drink and snack vending machines. These are additional ways to increase your profits.

There are many other ways to generate income from real estate. I encourage you to become creative and consider different ways to increase your revenue.

CHAPTER 5 SUMMARY

- Five things make a property rent: price, timing, terms, location, and condition

- The property you are renting must be in top-notch condition.

- Location is the most essential thing in real estate, but it is not everything. If your location is not great or has changed for the worse, you can still rent your unit at some price.

- Overly restrictive terms of a lease can reduce or eliminate your market for tenants

- Pets are a part of the rental business. Find a way to live with them and profit from them.

- You can't time the market, so do not try. But there are natural times that are better to rent throughout a year than others. Know what those times are in your market.

- Price can overcome almost any negative with your rental home. Test the market by starting a little high and make adjustments every few days until you get the activity you want.

- Be prepared to negotiate with prospects before, during, and after a tenancy. Sometimes to take a little less for a longer-term or to secure a good tenant is better than stubbornly sticking to your price.

- Be sure to advertise your properties for rent in multiple media sources. Emphasize internet advertising, where most prospects look for properties for rent.

- Rent is not the only source of income available to investment property owners. Search your market and be creative and consider other options to earn money on your rental home.

CHAPTER 6

TRAINING TENANTS

*R*onnie *and Tonya Herrell own a baker's dozen of rental homes. They began investing in real estate about four years ago and have had an outstanding experience so far. Each time one becomes vacant, they both take off work for a week to get the unit in top-notch condition, show the property, evaluate the price, and otherwise do what it takes to get the property rented. They enjoy getting down and dirty in the rental property business. It's a nice break from their accounting and nursing day jobs. Many times, they have even had their units re-rented within the week they took off.*

While painting their vacant duplex on Forrest Drive, a prospective renter noticed their yard sign and stopped.

"Can I take a look?" asked the man as his family waited in the car.

"Sure," Tonya said. "It's a three-bedroom house with two baths. We're asking $1,100 a month for it. Feel free to look around, but be careful. There is wet paint".

"Thanks, we will," he said, as he motioned for his wife and children to join him.

Tonya reached over and turned down the music playing on her iPhone and yelled, "Ronnie, there are some people looking at the house."

"No problem," Ronnie called back from down the hall. They were accustomed to showing the house while they worked. Tonya went back to cutting in the paint around the baseboard in the living room.

Ten minutes later, the prospect popped back into the living room and said, "We like it, but are you going to do something about the refrigerator?"

The refrigerator was only three years old, and although it was not spotless, it was in pretty good shape.

"We'll make sure it is cleaned up before someone moves in," Tonya said. "We're not quite finished with the house yet."

"When will it be ready?" he asked.

"We should be done by Friday afternoon," said Tonya. "The carpet cleaner is scheduled to be here then. How long have you been looking for a home?"

"Only a couple of weeks, but they are hard to find in this neighborhood," he said.

"Yes, I know," Tonya replied. "That's what attracted us to this property in the first place."

Ronnie walked in and introduced himself.

"I'm Ronnie Herrel," he said. "I'd shake your hand, but mine is covered in paint."

"No problem, I understand," said the man. "I'm Jeff Gibbons, and *this is my wife Rene, and my sons, Jeff Jr., and Jack."*

"It's nice to meet you," said Ronnie. "Would you like an application?"

"Sure, can we take it with us, and think about it?" Jeff said.

"No problem. If we're not here when you return, just seal the completed application in an envelope along with a $40 application fee, and leave it in the mailbox," instructed Ronnie. "We'll be here most of the week."

"Thanks," said Jeff. "I think we'll look around the back yard before we leave."

"Okay, let us know if you have any questions," Tonya replied.

The Gibbons' shuffled out the front door, and Ronnie and Tonya went back to work.

The next morning when they returned to the house, Ronnie checked the mailbox. Inside was an envelope with the name "Gibbons" printed on the front. Ronnie opened it and found the completed application along with a check for $40.

"The Gibbons' turned in their application," he said to Tonya.

"Awesome!" Tonya replied, while unlocking the front door.

The house smelled of fresh paint and cleaning supplies. It would soon be ready for tenants.

"I'll be in in a minute," Ronnie said. "I'm going to start running the application."

Ronnie went back to the truck and retrieved his iPad. After logging onto the screening service provider's website, he entered the Gibbons' information and waited for the results. Their average credit score was 730 — much higher than they were used to — with no judgments, collections, or evictions. The address history consisted of a short list, which Ronnie copied down. He logged onto the tax assessor's website and identified the landlords of the previous addresses.

One by one, Ronnie called and left messages for the landlords. He was happy to see that he knew one of them through the local Real Estate Investors Club. That landlord answered on the second ring.

After a few pleasantries, Ronnie began asking about the Gibbons family.

"In a lot of ways, I hate to lose them," he said. "They have always paid on time and take good care of the property."

"What about the other ways?" Ronnie asked.

"I don't know," he said, with an almost audible shrug. "I guess they always seemed a little needy."

That doesn't sound that bad, Ronnie thought.

"Anything else?" he asked.

"Not really," said his friend.

Ronnie told him he was looking forward to seeing him at the Real Estate Investors Club's next meeting and ended the call.

"So far, it looks pretty good," he told Tonya, as he entered the house.

"*I left a couple of messages for some other landlords, but I talked to a good one already. They also have a 730 credit score.*"

"*So, what are we waiting for?*" *Tonya said.* "*Let's take them before someone else does.*"

"*Let's give it until at least this afternoon,*" *said Ronnie.* "*We still have a lot of work to do here.*"

"*Okay, that sounds good,*" *Tonya said and got back to work.*

After an exhausting day working on the duplex, they arrived home that evening around 6. Ronnie tapped in the Gibbons' number on his iPhone and waited for an answer. Jeff answered promptly. After cordial introductions between the two men, Ronnie informed him of the successful application and asked when he would like to move in.

"*We would like to move in about two weeks,*" *Jeff said.* "*I need to give my current landlord 30 days' notice, so that should give us time to get moved.*"

"*That doesn't sound like a problem,*" *Ronnie said.* "*We will have the house ready by then. Can you come by tomorrow and bring the deposit?*"

"*Sure, I'll swing by around 9:00,*" *Jeff said.*

"*Tonya and I will be working there all day tomorrow,*" *said Ronnie.* "*Come by anytime.*"

Shortly before nine the next morning, Jeff came by as promised.

"*Thanks for giving us this opportunity,*" *he said.* "*I really appreciate it."*

"We're looking forward to having you as one of our residents," said Ronnie. "Would you like to help me remove the 'for rent' sign?"

"Nah, I have to head to work," he said. "I'll see you in a couple of weeks."

After the Gibbons family moved in, Tonya was filing all their paperwork and began to notice how picky they had been on their move-in check sheet.

"They noted four dozen items on their checklist," she said to Ronnie. "Look at how small some of these are: 'small spot on electrical outlet in living room, ceiling fan in bedroom is a little wobbly, and area under staircase not painted well.'"

"They have probably been burned by a bad landlord before and just wanted to cover all their bases," said Ronnie.

"You're probably right," she said.

The calls began two weeks later.

"When are you going to take care of that wobbly ceiling fan?" Jeff asked Ronnie.

"I didn't know you had a problem with it," Ronnie said.

"I put it on my move-in check sheet," he said.

"I thought you were just noting that," explained Ronnie. "I didn't know it was a problem. I'll come by and look at it this evening."

"Thanks," Jeff said. "Are you going to paint under the stairwell *also?"*

"Well, I wasn't planning on it, but I'll look to see if I have any paint left," said Ronnie. "If so, I'll take care of it."

"Thanks," Jeff said. "See you tonight."

Ronnie did not arrive home until after 11 that night.

"Where have you been?" Tonya demanded.

"Forrest Drive!" Ronnie snapped right back. "Every time I turned around, they wanted something else done."

"Like what?" she asked. "We left it in great shape."

"Yeah, that's what I thought, but listening to them, it might as well have been a pigsty," said Ronnie.

Two evenings later, Rene Gibbons called Tonya.

"I think there might be mice in the attic," she said.

"What makes you think that?" Tonya asked.

"Jack and Jr. thought they heard something last night," she said.

"Ok, I'll see what I can do," Tonya said.

Tonya didn't think the call was urgent, failed to mention it to Ronnie, and promptly forgot about it.

A few days later, Jeff called Ronnie. Jeff was furious because no one had taken action on the mice problem.

"When are you going to take care of that mice problem?" he

shouted.

"What mice problem?" Ronnie asked.

"Rene called Tonya about it three days ago!" Jeff said.

"I don't know what she's done about it," Ronnie said. "Let me check, and I'll get back to you. I didn't notice any mice or droppings when I was working over there. What makes you think you have mice?"

"My kids heard them Monday night," Jeff said.

"Have you heard them since?" Ronnie asked.

"Not that I know of, but I want someone to check it out," Jeff demanded.

"All right, I'll check it out," Ronnie said.

When Ronnie confronted Tonya, she said, "I'm so sorry, I forgot all about it. I really didn't think it was that big of a deal."

"Well, I don't either, but they're ticked now," he said. "I'll go climb in the attic and take a look."

"You know there are no mice there," Tonya said. "We would have seen evidence of them when we were going through the unit."

"I know, but I'm going to go over there and try to mend the fence," he said.

"I'll go with you," Tonya said.

Once at the house, Ronnie climbed into the attic and looked carefully for any signs of mice. He found nothing of concern. He came *back downstairs and reported to the Gibbons family that the house was mice free.*

"How do you know?" Jeff insisted. "You're not a pest control expert."

Jeff's outburst was the last straw for Ronnie.

"Look, enough is enough," Ronnie said, making every effort to control his temper. "We have already bent over backward for you in this house. There are no mice in the attic. The ceiling fan was not wobbly enough for concern. And no one is going to be under the stairwell, so repainting it was futile. In the future, please refrain from calling us for such minor issues that are really no problem in the first place."

"Wait a minute," Jeff began. "We pay good money to live here and expect..."

"If we are not living up to your expectations, please feel free to find alternative housing," said Ronnie sternly, abruptly cutting him off. "Otherwise, we will make sure all of your essential services are in good working order, and you have a safe, habitable house. If you have concerns about these issues, call us, and we'll take care of them right away. Otherwise, take care of it yourself or ignore it altogether."

The next several months went by smoothly. There was a main sewer line problem that Ronnie was happy to address as soon as he heard about it, but other than pleasantries when Jeff paid his rent, there were no other communications between them. Things were finally running well with all 13 of the Herrel's units.

There is a fine line between customer service and allowing tenants to take advantage of you. Sometimes you will need to find that line, expose it, and enforce it. Begin by setting expectations with your residents before they move in. Here are some ways that may help establish a good relationship.

MAINTENANCE CALLS

Maintenance is the most common way for tenants to take advantage of a landlord. There are many things good landlords should address without being asked and some that are opportunities to exceed your tenants' expectations. But other items simply do not warrant attention. Develop your maintenance procedures in writing. Include how tenants should make a maintenance request when they can expect return communications or action on a maintenance request, and detailed emergency procedures. Have residents review this document and sign it before they move into your property.

Be sure to include a general idea of the items for which you accept responsibility, and be clear what you consider "minor concerns" that may be taken care of in the future, or that the tenant can take care of if they wish. Generally, a landlord maintains the "systems" of a home (plumbing, electrical, gas, roof, appliances) and its habitability. The tenants are typically responsible for the day-to-day general maintenance of the house (cleaning, flipping breakers, or resetting ground fault indicator (GFI) plugs, plunging plumbing) or damage they may have caused on their own. Ensure the residents are aware they will be charged for a repair to a system if they were the cause for the failure.

Let's face it; some people do not know how to do simple things around a house, like pushing a reset button on a GFI plug or changing a smoke detector battery. Create simple videos that you can send to your tenants when a request like this comes in. The video can simply be you illustrating how to perform a specific task. You can also find videos like this on YouTube and send the tenant a link to that video.

You may prefer to attend to some general maintenance items for liability reasons. For example, you never want to require tenants to climb a ladder. There are too many risks of injury. Therefore, you may wish to remain responsible for cleaning gutters or changing fixtures (light bulbs, smoke detector batteries, etc.), or other chores that require the use of something taller than a step ladder.

If you are going to negotiate maintenance items, make them clear either in the maintenance document or, better yet, in the lease. Lawn care is a good example. Make sure you and your tenants know who is responsible for it. Once again, from a liability standpoint, do not provide them with a lawnmower or other tools. If you do, you could be responsible if there is an injury to a tenant or damage to property.

HONEYMOON PERIOD

Just like with any relationship, there is a period when a tenant and landlord are getting to know each other. I call the first 30 days the "Honeymoon Period." The honeymoon period is when you find out how needy they are, and they learn if you are going to be responsive to their needs.

The first month is also when the tenant finds all the things wrong with a house that a landlord could not identify without actually living in the house. Except for urgent repairs, be sure to have the new tenants keep a list of small repairs needed for the first 30 days and return it to you. This way, you can take care of all the issues at once instead of sending someone to work on the property every other day.

LEASE REQUIREMENTS

Promptly address lease violations, especially those that occur early in the tenancy period. Set the expectation that you are going to honor your end of the bargain, but you expect them to do the same. For example, if they are responsible for utilities and they have not turned them on in the first couple of days, do not delay. Confront them immediately. Advise them of their responsibility, and take action if they do not comply.

Late payments are another commonly ignored issue. If you have a good tenant and want to give them a break on one late payment, that is OK, but do not just waive the fee without letting the tenant know that future late payments are unacceptable. You want to be clear that you intend to enforce the lease, including late fees and any other penalties you may have specified in your lease. If you ignore it once, it could become an expectation that you ignore it again.

FIRM BUT POLITE

How you enforce a lease or contract is just as important as the terms. When making demands on people, you must be firm to get your point across, but you also must be polite. It does not matter what they say. If they are calling you names or complaining about the way you do business, do not get argumentative, and never use foul or insulting language. Stick to your guns and kill them with kindness.

We have all been in those circular conversations where you will say one thing and the other angry person will offer their opinion. The two of you keep coming back to the same thing over and over again. These are very difficult to end, and often the disagreements will spiral out of control. Once again, it is vitally important that you maintain your composure and be polite. When you see the conversation is not likely to end, do not just hang up on them (or walk away if it is in person). Hanging up on them is like throwing gasoline on a fire. It infuriates your adversary even more. State something along the lines of "We'll just have to agree to disagree." Typically, they will return to their argument, at which time you can politely reply, "We'll just have to agree to disagree" again. Do this as many times as it takes for the tenants to recognize that continuing the argument is pointless.

CHAPTER 6 SUMMARY

- Provide excellent customer service, but do not let tenants take advantage of you.

- Specify your maintenance procedures and expectations in writing and have the tenants sign them.

- Beware of requiring tenants to do something that could be considered dangerous. You could be responsible for injuries if they get hurt.

- Expect a 30-day "honeymoon period" where you and your tenants develop your relationship and learn about each other.

Set the expectation of high customer service within your responsibilities.

- Enforce lease violations timely. If you let it go once, you could build the expectation that you are going to let it go again.

- Be firm but polite in adversarial situations.

CHAPTER 7

AVOIDING LAWSUITS

*T*here's practically no risk to owning a rental property," Tony said, as he attempted to talk Jim into investing his latest bonus from work into a real estate venture. "You won't have to worry about a thing. I'll take care of everything. I'll collect the rent, find the tenants, and take care of the maintenance. All you have to do is put up the money, and we can share equally in the profits."

Looking up from his third drink, Jim finally conceded.

"All right, I was just going to put the bonus into my 401K anyway," he said. "Why not?"

Three years and two tenants had passed since then. For the most part, things had run smoothly. Tony had asked Jim for more investment funds only one time, and it was when a compressor went out in the air-conditioning system. Other than that, it had been a profitable experience. The pair had paid three years on their 15-year mortgage. Things were looking up.

Then, Tony received a letter in the mail from their tenants, giving their 30-day notice to move. Scrolling through his contacts on his cell phone, he found Jim's information and tapped the screen to call him. Jim answered on the third ring.

"Hey Jim, it's Tony," he said.

"Uh oh, this can't be good," Jim said.

"Well, it's not that bad," Tim said. "I just wanted you to know that I received a 30-day notice from our tenant. I'll place an ad on Craigslist tomorrow morning and see what kind of interest I can get. I believe the property will be in pretty good shape."

"Oh, okay," Jim said with a sigh of relief. "I was afraid you needed some more money from me."

"I don't think so," Tony replied. "We have some funds in our account, and I'll do most of the work to get the house ready myself."

"Great," said Jim. "Let me know how it goes."

As Tony placed his ad, he remembered how much damage the previous tenants' pets did. He decided to rewrite the ad to exclude pets.

He was surprised how much activity he received on the house right away. Within 24 hours, he had 16 calls. Some of the callers wanted to put in an application without even seeing the property.

Tony contacted the current tenants and arranged to show the property on Saturday between 11 a.m. and noon. He invited all of the prospects to join him to see the interior of the home.

"I know I have at least three people coming on Saturday," Tony reported to Jim.

"Good," said Jim. "Did you go up on the rent?"

"I sure did, and my phone is still ringing off the hook!" he bragged.

"Maybe we can make this house more profitable," said Jim.

Tony arrived early on Saturday. Two prospective tenants — one man and one woman — were already waiting on him in cars parked on the side of the street. He waved at both vehicles as he walked to the front door. The prospects stepped out of their cars, and Tony motioned for them to wait.

"Hang on just a moment, please," he said. "Let me make sure no one is home first."

The prospects nodded their understanding and mingled around the front yard, waiting in gorgeous September sunshine.

Tony pulled the key from his pocket and unlocked the door. No lights were on inside the house as he opened the door.

"Landlord!" he yelled into the empty foyer. Hearing nothing, he stepped inside and began turning on the lights.

"Landlord!" he yelled up the steps, just in case someone did not hear him the first time.

Satisfied that nobody was home, he poked his head out the front door and told the prospects they could come inside.

As the prospects began to roam through the house, Tony noticed it was not as clean as he would have liked. But it was almost presentable.

"What are you going to do to the place?" the lady asked.

"I'll make sure the house is clean, apply a fresh coat of paint, and clean the carpets before someone moves in," Tony said.

The gentleman continued his tour of the home but obviously did not like what he saw. Turning his nose up, he walked out the front door without even saying goodbye. Noticing the man leaving, the woman descended the stairs and approached Tony.

"I see your ad says 'No Pets,'" she said. "Do you have any flexibility in that?"

"Absolutely not!" said Tony. "For that matter, I'd prefer no kids either."

"I understand," she said. "I lost my husband in a car accident last year. My daughter has a small, two-year-old Maltese that her doctor says helps her through the stress in day-to-day living with the loss of her father."

"I'm sorry for your loss, but I just don't want any pets in this house," Tony said. "Pets almost destroyed my house the last time I allowed them."

"Okay, thank you," she said dejectedly. "May I have an application anyway?"

"Sure," Tony said, as he handed her an application. He wondered why she would take one knowing she would not qualify.

The woman thanked Tony and walked out of the front door. He hung around for another 45 minutes. In that time, he had six more prospects walk through the house, and four of them took applications.

On Monday, Tony had two applications returned to him. The first was from a young couple who had impressed him as excellent tenant prospects. They were just getting started in their careers, so their income was a little low. But they had no children and no animals. Furthermore, he recognized their family name — Ferguson — as one of the prominent families in the area.

The second application surprised him. It was from the woman who had asked about the pets. The application included the following cover letter:

To: Whom It May Concern

From: Diana Leonard

Dear Sir or Madam:

My daughter suffers from post-traumatic stress syndrome after being involved in a car accident that took her father's life. Her health and quality of life are vastly improved as long as she has her pet Maltese named "Boo." I know you do not want pets in your home, but I promise you this animal will do no damage to your home. If it does, I will pay for it.

As you can see from our completed application, I have been in my job for more than 15 years and have excellent landlord references. We would not even be moving if it had not been for the car accident. Please find it in your heart to allow us to rent your home.

Thank you for your consideration,

Diana Leonard and Stephanie Leonard

The package also included a signed note from Stephanie's doctor, on his letterhead, re-stating the need for Stephanie's "comfort animal."

The application itself was complete and included Diana's two most recent pay stubs from her employer. She made ample money to qualify for the home.

Tony was conflicted about this situation, so he began the background checks on both applicants. He hoped that he could find some other reason to deny the Leonards' application. After completing his due diligence, however, the only reason he could find to refuse them was Boo.

Tony met Jim the next morning to discuss the situation.

"I really don't want a pet in the house," Tony pointed out.

"Yeah, but she makes a lot more money than the other applicants, and she promised to pay for any damage caused by the dog," Jim said.

"Come on," Tony said. "We've heard promises before. You know as well as I do that you can't buy anything with promises. They just seem to cost you more money."

"But the other applicant doesn't even earn two and half times the rent," Jim said. "How are they going to pay for it?"

"They're Fergusons!" Tony responded. "If it was necessary, we could get it from their family."

"Good point," said Jim. "It's hard to go wrong with Fergusons."

"And they don't have any pets or kids."

"Let's go with them," Tony agreed.

Tony called the Fergusons and informed them they could have the home. They were very excited and began to make plans to move in early in the month.

He didn't look forward to making the next call, but he had a mentor tell him to *"attack the dragon while it is small,"* so he didn't put it off.

"Ms. Leonard?" Tony asked after a woman answered the phone.

"Yes?" she said.

"Hello, this is Tony," he said. *"I met you on Sunday."*

"Oh, yes," she replied. *"How did you like my application?"*

"I'll admit that your landlord references and your job history looked very good, but I had another application that I liked better," he said. *"I accepted it."*

"What did you like better about it?" she asked.

"To be honest, it was just what I told you on Sunday," he explained. *"They don't have any kids or pets. They were simply a better fit for the home."*

Tony could hear the frustration building on the other end of the line.

"After looking at my references, you have to know that we would be great tenants, even with my daughter and her dog," she said as calmly as she could. *"This reason is unacceptable."*

"I'm really sorry for your situation, but I have to look out for my property," Tony said.

"You will be hearing from my lawyer!" she said.

"I'm sorry you feel that way," Tony replied. "I hope you find an acceptable property."

"I already have, and you are standing in my way to it!" Dianna barked and hung up the phone.

The end of the month came, and Tony could not wait for the tenants to get out of the house. He was eager to get the house ready for the Fergusons to move in. The keys were turned in by 2 p.m. on the 30th, just as Tony had requested.

He raced over to the house, inserted the key, and unlocked the door. He quickly scanned the house, room by room, noting the following items:

- *Nail holes in living room walls*

- *Carpet not clean throughout house*

- *Oven dirty*

- *Bathtub in hall bath dirty*

- *Wear on carpet in hallway*

- *Sink faucet in hall bathroom is dripping*

As he was finishing his walkthrough, Kyle, Tony's go-to handyman contractor, showed up. As they greeted one another and shook hands, Tony explained the situation.

"I have some folks moving in as soon as I can get it ready," said Tony. "How long will it take you?"

Kyle walked through the house, tallying up the repairs and cleaning as he went. Some 10 minutes later, he provided an estimate of $700 to get the house ready.

"They left it in pretty good shape," Kyle remarked. "It should only take me a couple of days. I'll start tomorrow since you already have someone lined up to move in."

"Man, $700 sounds like a lot," Tony said, as he looked at the estimate.

"I know," said Kyle. "Blame it on the workman's comp insurance. It is sky-high."

"Oh well, I'll take it out of the security deposit," Tony said with a shrug. "That will be that much less I need to refund to them."

Kyle got to work as promised the next day, and Tony mailed a check to the former tenants for the remainder of the security deposit.

As promised, the house was ready in a couple of days, and Tony moved the Fergusons in. The young couple could not have been happier to get the home.

Two days later, Tony received a call from the former tenants. "Why did you deduct $700 from our security deposit?" the gentleman demanded.

"That's what it cost me to get the house ready for the next tenants," Tony explained.

"No way," he protested. "We cleaned the heck out of the house. We left you almost nothing to do!"

"I had to touch up the paint, clean the carpets, repair a faucet drip, and clean the oven," Tony explained. "That was not the way I left it for you when you moved in."

After some more back and forth in the conversation, the former tenant said, "You'll be hearing from my lawyer!" and hung up.

Three months had gone by when Tony heard a knock on his front door. Leaving the comfort of his sofa, he walked to the door and peered through the peephole. It was the mailman, so Tony opened the door.

"Certified mail for you, sir," the mail carrier said as he held out a clipboard. "Please sign here."

Tony signed it, thanked the mailman, and closed the front door. Knowing that nothing good ever comes from certified mail, he looked at the envelope anxiously. It was from the local legal aid society. Using his index finger, he tore open the envelope. The letter was formal and direct. He immediately picked up the phone and called Jim.

Jim had just received a similar certified letter as well.

"What's up?" Jim asked.

"The former tenants' lawyer is demanding that we return the remaining $700, plus another $1,400 for something called 'treble damages' plus a $300 fee to his firm for their services," Tony said. "He cited some state law that requires landlords to account for normal wear and tear.".

"Is he right?" said Jim.

"I don't know," said Tony. "I have always just kept what I thought was right from a security deposit."

"I have a friend who is a lawyer," Jim offered. "Maybe she can give us some advice."

Later that evening, Jim went to Tony's house to discuss the matter.

"I noticed that the letter said they would like to audit our security deposit account as well," said Jim.

"Yeah, what do they mean by that?" Tony asked.

"According to the lawyer I spoke with today, who admitted that landlord-tenant law was not her specialty, we are supposed to hold security deposits in escrow," Jim said. "Where have you kept the security deposit in the past?"

"I just deposit them into our business account," Tony said. Frankly, sometimes the security deposits have kept me from having to ask you for more money to fund the account."

"I'm afraid we may be in trouble," Jack said. "That letter may be right. We will have to refund them that $700. Let's just hope we can negotiate our way out of the treble damages."

"What should we do now?" Tony asked.

"I'm not sure, but I suggest we hire our own attorney to handle it," Jim said.

"I wonder what that's going to cost," Tony said.

"We'll find out in the morning," said Jim. "You are going to find an attorney who specializes in landlord-tenant law."

"Okay, I'll begin work on that tonight," Tony agreed.

After googling local attorneys, Tony settled on Eric Smith, whose office was downtown. He called Mr. Smith's office the next morning and the receptionist scheduled an appointment for 1 p.m. the next day.

The next day, Tony arrived at the law office 10 minutes early. Still, he had to wait 40 minutes before the attorney could see him. When Tony was finally ushered into the lawyer's posh office, he quickly explained his predicament.

"First things first, if they learn that you have miscounted for the security deposit, you will have no right to any of it," said Smith. "Furthermore, by co-mingling the funds with your business, you could be charged with fraud. That is a jailable crime."

"I had no idea I was doing anything wrong!" Tony exclaimed.

"Don't worry," said Smith. "I'm not going to let it get that far, but it is going to cost you. I will need $500 to start, and I bill at $150 an hour. My office will bill you once a week. I expect this to be a simple negotiation with the other attorney, so the $500 may cover it all. But be prepared to pay a settlement to the former tenants and their legal fees."

"Okay," Tony said as he reluctantly pulled out his checkbook and wrote the $500 check. "Please keep me informed."

Tony walked out of the lawyer's office with a dejected expression on his face. He quickly phoned Jim to give him the bad news.

"Are you serious?" Jim asked.

"Unfortunately, I am," said Tony. "I think I screwed up pretty bad, but I learned my lesson. It won't happen again."

"Yeah, you learned your lesson on my dime!" Jim retorted. "I'm sorry to yell at you. This is not the only problem I'm dealing with right now. My wife called about an hour ago saying a process server came by the house to serve me a summons. There's no telling what that is all about."

"Oh, I'm sorry," said Tony. "I'll try to make this as easy as possible."

When Tony arrived home, he immediately settled onto the couch in front of the TV, not really watching it, just stewing in his thoughts. The doorbell rang, shattering his peace. Tony opened the door to find a large, gruff-looking man in jeans and a Van Halen T-shirt on his front porch."

"Can I help you?" Tony asked.

"I have a summons for Tony Saragossa," the man said in a deep voice.

"That's me," he said.

The man jammed a yellow piece of paper into Tony's hand.

"You've been served," he said and then turned to walk away.

"What's this all about?" Tony asked.

"Hell if I know," he said, as he slammed the door on his old, beat-up truck. "I just deliver the bad news."

Under the front porch light, Tony looked in his hands at the yellow paper. He read the word "summons" across the top. As Tony continued to read, it was from a court in the capital requiring him to appear at 9 a.m. in three weeks. Reading further, he found that a fair housing complaint had been filed against him.

"What next?" Tony thought.

Remembering that Jim had said he was served one of these this morning, he picked up the phone and called him.

"I got served as well," Tony said into the receiver.

"What's it all about?" Jim asked. *"He couldn't leave it with my wife, so he told her he would be back later."*

"Apparently someone has filed a fair housing complaint against us," Tony said.

"What the heck is that?" Jim said.

"It has something to do with discrimination," Tony explained.

"Discrimination?" Jim exclaimed. *"I don't discriminate...hang on, my doorbell just rang."*

A few minutes later, he picked up the phone and said, *"I just got served."*

"Maybe we should go back and talk to that lawyer again tomorrow," Tony said.

"Good idea," Jim agreed. *"This time, I'm going with you."*

The next afternoon, they met at Mr. Smith's office for a 2 p.m. appointment. After a few pleasantries, Mr. Smith said, *"I have some good news. I was able to reach the other lawyer about the security deposit.*

It's a young kid working with the legal aid society for free unless he can get a defendant to pay him. Anyway, he thinks they will agree to cut the damages in half. You will have to pay the $700 security deposit back, $700 in damages, and his fee of $300."

"Holy cow!" said Tony. "That's $1,700! Is that the best we can get?"

"Not necessarily, but if you end up in court, you are most likely going to lose," he said. "The damages will be more, and my legal fees and theirs will be higher, too. I believe it is in your best interest to take this deal. Keep in mind; I don't have this on paper yet, just a brief conversation this morning."

Jim looked at Tony and nodded.

"Okay, let's just put this behind us," Jim said.

"Mr. Smith, that is not all we have to discuss," said Tony. "We received these summonses yesterday and don't know what to do with them."

Reading the summons through his reading glasses, Mr. Smith said, "Uh oh, this isn't good. This is a fair housing complaint."

"What does that mean?" said Tony. "We don't discriminate against anyone."

"That's not necessarily true," said Smith. "For instance, you may discriminate against someone with no job or bad landlord references or someone who has pets. For the most part, that is okay. But there are seven protected classes that you cannot discriminate against for any

reason."

Mr. Smith continued with a brief explanation of the Federal Fair Housing Act and the state laws that go with it.

"The complaint states that you discriminated against the handicap and familial status protected class," the attorney said.

"What the heck does that mean?" asked Tony.

"Handicap is self-explanatory," he said. "You may have turned down someone in a wheelchair, someone who is blind, or with some other disability. Many times they aren't so obvious. Familial status has to do with how big the family is and the make-up of it. You couldn't restrict most homes from children."

Tony looked down at the floor and mumbled, "Uh-oh."

"Can you recall what that may have been, Tony?" asked Mr. Smith.

"Yes, I might know," Tony said and proceeded to explain about the Leonard family application, which he denied because she had the pet and a child when the other applicants didn't have either.

"This is definitely not good," the lawyer said. "I'll need to look further into this complaint. For now, put that appearance date on your calendar and plan to be there. With fair housing, we are dealing with the federal government. You are either guilty or not. There is no in-between. From what you have told me, you are guilty. Be prepared to say that and take whatever punishment they mete out. I'll do what I can. I hate to add insult to injury, but this will take a lot more of my time. I'm going to need another $1,000 to get started on this for you."

Tony wrote another check, stood up, and shook Mr. Smith's hand as they said goodbye.

Three days later, Mr. Smith called Tony with the settlement they expected with the former tenants. Tony and Jim had to pay $1,400 to them, plus $300 to their lawyer. The fair housing complaint was still looming.

The attorney finally contacted Tony again with only four days before they were due to appear in court.

"I'm afraid there is not much we can do about the fair housing complaint," he said. "All we can do is plead your ignorance and hope they don't go too hard on you because this is your first offense."

On the day of their court date, they arrived at the federal courthouse in the capital. They sat in a large, dark courtroom awaiting their turn. Tony noticed the Leonards on the third pew watching the proceedings and glaring at Tony from time to time. When it was their turn, Tony explained to the judge that he did not know that he was doing anything improper, as Mr. Smith advised him. The judge chastised Tony and Jim for their ignorance and lectured them on what they had done wrong.

"The maximum fine for a fair housing violation is $250,000," said the judge. "I mention this to let you know that even though your fine is going to be significant, it could have been a lot worse. Your fine will be $15,000 to be paid in 30 days."

The size of the fine was no surprise to Tony and Jim. Mr. Smith had already warned them of the hefty penalties for violating fair housing, but it still hurt.

The judge adjourned court and everyone began to file out of the room. Tony noticed Diana Leonard and walked up to her. Diana saw him approaching and took a defensive stance.

"I just wanted to say I'm sorry," said Tony. "It never occurred to me how hard it might be for some folks to find housing. I never meant to hurt you or anyone else."

Diana relaxed a bit and said, "I accept your apology and offer you forgiveness."

Forgiveness took a little of the sting out of the fine for Tony. They shook hands and parted in separate directions down the hall.

Guilty! That is one word you do not want to have to say when standing in a dark, wood-paneled courtroom, just beyond the half swinging door, to the man or woman, who sits three feet above you, wearing a well-pressed black robe. Guilty quickly translates into expensive. Fines, damages, punitive action, etc., can add up to thousands of dollars.

You may have heard it your entire life, but ignorance is no excuse for breaking the law. You must understand the rules you must comply with to be a landlord. It is equally important to keep up to date as regulations change or are added to the books. When you accidentally break one, it can be very costly.

We cannot possibly do an extensive study on all the laws that could affect your business. Therefore, we will briefly go over a few that are most likely to get you in trouble, starting with your local jurisdictions.

LOCAL LAWS AND ORDINANCES

There are thousands of counties, parishes, and municipalities in this country. Each has a little different way of doing things. Learn who the players are in your area. Speak with them to determine what you can expect in an eviction proceeding, security deposit dispute, or if there are rental registration requirements in that area. If you do business in multiple areas, you may need different leases and have different legal procedures to comply with each. Be sure to understand their idiosyncrasies before your next legal challenge.

Rental registration is something that is sweeping the nation now. Many local governments require landlords to register their properties they rent with the building and codes department or whatever entity they task with the responsibility. Usually, there is a small fee associated with the registration, but it is much less than the penalties for not registering when required.

Many locations, especially those in rural areas, do not even have many of their rules in writing. They are passed down over the years through case precedence. It is crucial to understand how the system works in your area.

STATE LAWS AND REGULATIONS

Most states will have laws or regulations their legislative body passed, likely many years ago, that will establish the rules of the game by which landlords and tenants must play. The state "Landlord and Tenant Act," or something similar, is usually what the laws will be titled. The title and the rules will vary from state to state. Some are very detailed, establishing the day-to-day guidelines that you must comply with as a landlord. Others are very vague and open to interpretation. Then some states do not have a landlord and tenant act at all. Even those will have laws with which you need to be familiar. Learn the rules in your state and study them carefully. The state law will dictate more about your business than probably any other level of government.

I know most people do not care about politics very much. But when it comes to the rental industry, the state imposes a lot of rules with which you must comply. Furthermore, these rules can change or be amended with little or no notice. Get to know your state legislators and keep in touch with them. For that matter, offer to help them when they get lost in landlord-tenant issues. After all, you are the expert.

One of the most significant sources of legal problems is the handling of security deposits. Be sure to understand the rules on how to account for and disburse security deposits. There are usually precise procedures on how to handle deposits. Do not co-mingle your funds. Remember, the security deposit is not your money. It belongs to the tenant, and it must be accounted for appropriately.

Get involved in a local real estate group. If there is not one in your area, then start one and be sure to have someone in charge of watching what your state lawmakers are doing.

FEDERAL LAWS AND REGULATIONS

There are countless federal laws concerning the rental business, so we will just hit the high points and the ones that have the most severe penalties.

FEDERAL FAIR HOUSING ACT (FFHA): This act was adopted in 1968 and has been amended many times since then. It essentially says you are not allowed to discriminate against any of the seven protected classes for any housing-related reason. Those protected classes include race, color, national origin, religion, sex, familial status, and handicap (many states may have additional protected classes as well). Most of us will say to ourselves: "I would not discriminate against anyone anyway." And most of us wouldn't, at least not intentionally. But you can accidentally violate the Fair Housing Act in your advertising and marketing or in statements you make on the phone. Be sure you thoroughly understand how the Fair Housing Act can affect you, and be prepared to comply. The maximum penalty for violating the Fair Housing Act is $250,000.

AMERICANS WITH DISABILITIES ACT (ADA): The Americans with Disability Act (ADA) goes hand in hand with the Fair Housing Act, prohibiting discrimination against persons with disabilities. A landlord is required to make reasonable accommodations to help disabled persons to rent one of their properties. For example, if applicants are in a wheelchair, then installing a ramp would be a reasonable accommodation. Most alterations to the interior of a property, including but not limited to ramps or door widening, are to be completed at the tenants' expense and are to be returned to the way they received the property at the tenants' expense upon termination of the lease. A landlord cannot require an increased security deposit, fees, or any other item that negatively impacts the tenants due to any of these alterations or expenses. A common violation of the ADA is not to allow pets when prospects have a mental or physical disability that is helped by having a pet. These animals are called "comfort," "assistance," or "service" animals and can be any kind of animal. A landlord can require written evidence of the need for the animal if they wish.

FAIR DEBT COLLECTIONS ACT: This act was passed in 1996 to prohibit abusive practices by debt collectors. As landlords, we often have to collect late rents or even from tenants who have skipped out on us. Debt collectors are not allowed to harass or abuse those they are trying to collect from and may not make any false or misleading representations. Furthermore, phone calls to a deficient debtor cannot be made during "unusual" hours. Generally, interpretation of this has been you can only contact them between the hours of 8 a.m. and 9 p.m. Monday through Saturday. You must not contact them on Sundays.

FEDERAL FAIR CREDIT REPORTING ACT (FCRA): The FCRA was passed in 1970 with many amendments since. It is a long piece of legislation, but the bottom line for landlords is that you must ensure any data that you collect from your applicants is kept private. You cannot share it with your office, maintenance personnel, another landlord, spouse, or anyone. A landlord is also required to provide an "adverse action letter" to any prospect that has received a decision from you that negatively impacts them financially. For example, if you turn a prospect down or require a higher than the normal security deposit, you are required to explain to them why, in writing, and let them know how they can get a copy of their credit report themselves.

SOLDIERS AND SAILORS CIVIL RELIEF ACT (SSCRA): Passed in 1918, the SSCRA requires landlords who are leasing to military personnel to let these individuals out of a lease if they receive orders for a permanent change of station (PCS), exiting military service, or an extended temporary duty (TDY). If you work in a military area, be sure to understand this law well.

ENVIRONMENTAL PROTECTION AGENCY (EPA): The EPA is a regulatory agency that can profoundly impact landlords. While they have many rules with which we must comply, there are two that affect landlords the most, both dealing with lead-based paint. The lead-based paint rules apply to any home built prior to 1978 when lead-based paint was officially banned. If you rent a unit constructed before that year, you must disclose what you know about the existence of lead-based paint to a prospective tenant before executing a lease. You can find the official disclosure form at www.EPA.Gov/lead. Second is the EPA Renovate Right Program. The Renovate Right Program outlines the specific procedures a landlord must go through to do significant construction on a home built before 1978, much of which must be done by certified contractors. You can find more details on the Renovate Right Program at the above website as well.

There are dozens, if not hundreds, of laws that can affect your business as a landlord. I have only touched on a few in this chapter, and I must reiterate that I have only given you a very brief explanation of these laws. They are dozens of pages long. I encourage you to understand them thoroughly.

TENANT UNIONS

I know many landlords who know and understand the law but make a conscious decision to violate them anyway. I have found they do this for one of three reasons:

They think it will cost them less money,

They feel they are above the law or that the law is stupid, and

They are counting on the tenants being ignorant of the law and not fighting their decisions.

You may win that gamble (and it is a gamble) more times than not when choosing to break the law. But when you get caught, it can be costly. These days the gamble often doesn't pay off, thanks to the abundance of free legal assistance available to your tenants.

Tenant unions are popping up throughout the country. Starting in San Francisco in the 1970s, a Tenant Union is a group of people held together to defend each other against abuse from landlords. They are a free advocate for tenants' rights.

Another tenant advocate that costs little or nothing is the Legal Aid Society. The Legal Aid Society does an excellent job of helping those in poverty when they feel a landlord is taking advantage of them. Many times the issues they are helping with are landlord-tenant disputes.

As you can see, it is easy for a tenant that you have wronged, intentionally or unintentionally, to receive advice on how to proceed against a landlord. The gamble of breaking the rules and hoping no one calls you on it is simply not worth it anymore.

CHAPTER 7 SUMMARY

- Be sure to understand how the legal system in your local area works and what expectations there are for landlords.

- Know your state laws, especially the landlord and tenant act.

- There are dozens of federal laws, so be sure to understand those that are easiest to violate.

- Do not ignore the law. There are many free opportunities for your tenants and prospects to come after you.

CHAPTER 8

MANAGEMENT

*F*rank got home from his office, where he worked as an accountant for a local health care firm, just in time to say hi to his two daughters and kiss his wife, Angela, before he had to head right back out.

"I don't know how late I'll be girls," he said, stepping into his garage. "Don't wait on me for dinner."

"Come on, Frankie!" Angela said. "You've been doing this a lot lately! Those houses are going to be the death of you."

"I know, I know, but I have to take care of this," he said. "It just can't wait."

Earlier that day, he had received a letter from the city, informing him that there was an inoperable car parked in the yard of his rental duplex. It said the city was going to fine him if he did not remove the automobile within five days. Frank attempted to call his tenant, but the number he had for them had been disconnected. Now he had to miss dinner with his family to make sure the tenants' removed their broken-down car from the property.

Frank now owned four buildings for a total of six units. It seemed to him (and Angela) that these investments were consuming way too much of his time.

"There has to be an easier way to do this," he said to himself, backing out of the driveway.

While stopped in traffic, Frank opened Facebook on his iPhone. Scrolling through some of the statuses, he saw a post from Ben, a friend who was in a local real estate investor group. Ben had posted pictures of himself and his family on the beach in South Florida. He knew that Ben had about 30 rental properties.

"How can he get away all the time like this?" Frank said to himself as he stared at the red traffic light. He made a mental note to himself to ask Ben how he did it.

Arriving at the property, the first thing he noticed was an old Chevrolet Malibu parked in the grass near the front door. The car had a license plate that had expired six months prior, a cracked windshield, a missing headlight, and there was more rust on it than paint. The car was obviously inoperable.

Frank knocked on the front door and waited. He could hear movement inside, but no one came to the door. He walked around back and knocked on the door under the carport. His tenant, Jerry, opened the door, wearing only a pair of boxer shorts, and holding a Pabst Blue Ribbon in his left hand and a lit cigarette in the other."

"Whassup, Frank?" he said.

Frank held out the letter from the city.

"I'm going to get fined if you don't remove the car in the front

yard," he explained.

"Oh, that's my new Malibu," said Jerry. "Don't worry about it. It's going to be as good as new as soon as I can get the money for a new engine. You'll see — she's gonna be sharp."

"Well, in the meantime, it can't sit there," Frank said. "You have to move her."

"She won't start," Jerry protested. "How am I supposed to move her?"

"How did you get her here in the first place?" Frank asked.

"Johnny dropped her off with his car hauler," Jerry answered, taking a draw from his cigarette.

"Well, I suspect Johnny can pick her up as well," Frank said.

"Come on, man!" Jerry shot back. "Cut me some slack!"

"I can't," said Frank. "It's not up to me. The city is going to fine me $500, plus $50 per day if you don't comply. If I get that fine, I'm going to charge it to you."

"All right, all right," Jerry said. "I'll figure out something. How long do I have?"

"The letter says five days, but it was mailed to me two days ago," said Frank.

"Okay, I'll call Johnny in the morning," Jerry promised.

Frank got back in his car and looked around the interior of his new BMW 535 and thought to himself: "I sure like the money I can make off *these rental properties, but this crap is for the birds." He put the car in drive and headed home.*

Dinner was cold when he got to the table, and Angela was helping the girls with their homework. While Frank ate, he watched a little TV and then went to bed, hoping he would not be called out again tomorrow night because of one of his rental properties.

The next morning, Frank dialed Ben from his office. After Ben answered, it was soon evident that he was still on vacation.

"Why don't you come down here and join me?" Ben said.

"Yeah, I saw your pictures on Facebook," Frank said. "I'd love to, but I just don't have time.".

"Come on, we have nothing but time," Ben said.

"Actually, that's what I want to talk to you about," Frank said. "I know you own a bunch of rental properties, and I see that you travel all the time. My properties seem to require constant attention. How do you do it?"

"Oh, that's easy," he said. "I pay someone else to do it."

"You mean like a property manager?" Frank asked.

"Exactly," said Ben.

"Isn't that expensive?" said Frank.

"Not relative to what I get out of it," said Ben. "Look, I have the same problems you have with rental properties, probably even more so. But here I am, lounging by the pool in Miami. My time is way too

valuable to waste on piddly details like clogged toilets."

"Do you worry that the property manager might take advantage of you?" said Frank.

"It took me a while to trust someone to take over," Ben admitted. "Trust is a hard thing to come by, but the company I'm using has been great. I go through their monthly statement to make sure, but I haven't found a reason not to trust them yet."

"Who do you use?" Frank asked.

"First City Property Management," he said. "I'll text you the number. Tell them I told you to call."

Ben and Frank exchanged a few more words before hanging up. Frank had only minutes to wonder if this sort of arrangement might work for him before his iPhone alerted him to a new text message. Sure enough, Ben had provided him with First City Property Management's contact information.

As Frank sat at his desk, he kept thinking about Ben's comments. Still, he could not bring himself to pay a property manager. After all, he bought these rental houses because they were tangible, hands-on investments, not some electronic share of a company over which he had no control. That was what he liked about the business. Why would he give up that control?

Frank went back to work. He was doing what he loved best, playing with numbers. After a couple of hours, he checked his email. In his inbox, there was a message from one of his tenants. The subject line read "EMERGENCY." Thinking one of his houses must be burning down, he quickly clicked on the message. It read: *"Our toilet has overflowed onto the bathroom floor. Please help ASAP."*

Shaking his head, he picked up the phone and called his tenant.

"How bad is it?" he asked.

"Well, we have towels around the base of the toilet now, but we can't use it," the tenant replied.

"Did you try to plunge it?" Frank asked.

"No, I wasn't sure I should," said the tenant.

"Please try that first," Frank said. *"If that fixes the problem, email me back and let me know. Don't call. I can't take personal calls at work. If I don't hear from you, I'll stop by on my way home this afternoon."*

"Thanks, Frank," the tenant said. *"I'll try to plunge it now."*

Frank hung up the phone and decided enough was enough. He hoped his tenant would email to tell him the plunging worked before he got off his next call. He dialed the number. On the other end of the line, he heard a pleasant woman's voice say, *"First City Property Management, may I help you?"*

He explained that Ben had told him to call, and he wanted to speak to Ben's property manager.

"Oh, Ben has been a great client for us," said the woman. *"He's an excellent landlord. His property manager is Lisa Carlyle. She is in the field now, but I'll put you through to her cell phone. Hold on just a minute."*

After saying, "Thank you," Frank heard the click of a transfer and then some pleasant elevator music. Less than two minutes later, he heard, "Good afternoon, this is Lisa."

"Good afternoon, Lisa," he replied. "My name is Frank. Ben recommended I call you. I have a handful of rental houses and am considering hiring a property manager. How much do you charge?"

"Hello, Frank," Lisa said. "I'm glad Ben told you to call me. What you will find is that I don't 'charge' anything, but I will earn a little of the gross income. Our systems will net you more money and time than doing it yourself. Tell me where your properties are located."

Lisa asked Frank for more details about Frank's experience with rental properties. How long he had owned rental properties, how many units he had, what was their condition, etc.?

"What is your chief concern?" Lisa finally asked.

"What do you mean?" said Frank.

"What would you like most to get out of my services?" Lisa explained.

"Well, of course, I'd like to make more money, but really I'm just tired of being called out to these houses all the time," he said. "I have a job and a family and just don't have time to give them."

"Then I have some good news," Lisa said. "I will most likely earn you more money, and I'm sure I'll free you up from those little headaches that go along with rental homes. Let's get together this afternoon, and I can go over my entire program."

"I'd like that, but it looks like I'm going to have to go fix a toilet when I get off this afternoon," Frank said.

"At one of your rental properties?" Lisa asked.

"Yes, I received an email this morning about it," he said.

"Perfect! I'd like to see what you own anyway," she said. "Why don't I meet you there? If you'd like, I'll bring one of our maintenance technicians to repair that toilet for you."

"That sounds like a good plan," Frank said. "I'll see you there at 4:30 this afternoon."

He gave her the address, then hung up. Frank checked his email one more time before leaving the office and did not see anything from his tenant. Resigning himself to fixing the toilet, he called Angela.

"I'm sorry, honey, but I've got to take care of an issue at a rental property this afternoon," he said. "I hope to be home by seven at the latest."

"All right, I'll take care of the girls and see you then," she replied pleasantly, but Frank could hear the disappointment in her voice.

Frank arrived at his rental house at 4:30 sharp. He noticed two vehicles parked on the road; a large white maintenance van marked "First City Property Management" and the other a relatively new white Buick SUV. A woman stepped out of the SUV, as Frank pulled into the driveway. The woman came over to him as he was getting out of his car.

"Hello, Frank, I'm Lisa," she said.

She was shorter than he expected — around 5'3" tall and petite. He thought a property manager would need to be a big, burly person.

"Nice to meet you," Frank said, offering his hand to shake hers.

"Let's go take care of this toilet issue," she said, motioning to the uniformed maintenance technician.

They knocked on the door, and the tenant promptly answered.

"Oh, hey, Frank," she said. "The plunger worked. It seems to be working fine now."

"You were supposed to let me know if you didn't need me to come by," Frank said, obviously exasperated.

"I'm so sorry," she said. "I completely forgot."

"You know, as long as we're here, why don't you let Bobby take a look," Lisa said, motioning to the maintenance technician.

"That's a good idea," Frank said.

While Bobby was working in the bathroom, Lisa and Frank took a tour of the house. Lisa pointed out a few items she would like to see done to the property, mostly deferred maintenance.

"You see, the bottom of this door is beginning to show some rot," she said. "If you don't get it painted right away, you will have to replace the door in the future."

"Yeah, I'm glad you pointed that out," said Frank.

"See, I'm saving you money already," Lisa said with a smile.

"I fished out some old construction debris out of the toilet," Bobby said as he came down the hall from the bathroom. *"It should work fine now."*

"That doesn't surprise me," Frank said. *"When it was empty a couple of months ago, Angela and I spent a week out here remodeling the bathroom."*

They all thanked the tenant and stepped into the front yard.

"I can take all of these things off your hands," Lisa promised. *"I'll make sure that door gets painted, the rent is collected, the paperwork is correct, and all the day-to-day details that go along with owning rental properties. I will make sure you follow all laws and regulations, and I will get the jobs done right the first time."*

"That sounds good to me," Frank replied. *"Where do I sign?"*

After finishing the paperwork, they made arrangements to get all the keys and the tenants' contact information to Lisa so she could get to work. Frank drove home, arriving earlier than expected.

"That was quick," Angela observed.

"Yes, I had a pro snake out the toilet," he said. *"He found some debris from when we remodeled it a couple of months ago."*

"I was afraid of that," she said. *"I noticed some stuff fall into the toilet when we pulled the cabinets out."*

"I have more good news," said Frank.

"What's that?" Angela asked.

"I won't be dealing with the rental properties in the evening anymore," he said.

"How did you manage that?" she said.

"I hired a property manager today," Frank confessed.

"It's about time!" Angela said with a sigh.

Eight months later, at an REI meeting, Ben asked Frank how the relationship with Lisa and the management company was going.

"She's great!" Frank said. "I love the fact that she lets me know when something is wrong and then magically takes care of it. I don't have to do anything."

"Has she made you more money?" Ben asked.

"Not yet, but I can see it coming," said Frank. "She has turned over one of my units for more money and renewed a couple of leases after making the tenants very happy. I have also had to spend a little on safety issues. I didn't have carbon monoxide detectors in a couple of units, and she insisted they be installed."

"She's right," Ben noted. "That's just one more good thing about having a property manager. They know the traps you can walk into that can cost you a boatload if you're not careful."

"Yeah, I get that," Frank said. "The best thing is I'm not missing important things like my girls' dance recitals or date nights with Angela."

"I like having more time to find more properties," Ben agreed. "That's where the money really is."

"Did I tell you I got a raise at work?" Frank added.

"No," Ben said. Congratulations!"

"Thanks," said Frank. "My boss came to me out of the blue and said I had been much more productive over the last few months. He even pinpointed the date at which he saw improvement. It was the day after I hired Lisa."

MORE MONEY, MORE TIME

Some things are more valuable than money. One of these is time. An investment in scattered-site rental properties is a business. It's more complicated than simply handing over a wad of cash to a financial advisor and hoping it will grow. You must treat it as a business. It must have its own bank account. You must prepare a profit or loss statement, create an annual budget, and have a chief executive officer (CEO) to run it. Most of the time, the CEO is the owner of the property, but it does not have to be. Many investors believe the best approach is to hire a CEO for the rental property business, a property manager.

DRAWBACKS OF HIRING A PROPERTY MANAGER

There are some drawbacks to hiring a property manager. The obvious one is the cost. Depending on the location, type of property, and how many units you have, your management will cost somewhere between 7 and 20 percent of the income on the property. The cost of management is not just the management fee, which can be a percentage of income or a flat fee. It also includes any other fees associated with management of the property (This does not include the cost of maintenance or evictions, but the property management company could include extra fees associated with maintenance or evictions here). There are literally dozens of fees a property manager can put in place, such as leasing fees, renewal fees, set up fees, inspection fees, etc. Be sure to understand the management contract thoroughly before you authorize it.

Control of the property is another issue. Many of us who purchase rental properties do so because we like to control our investments. With Real Estate Investment Trusts, bonds, mutual funds, etc., you are unable to exercise much control. Control is what attracts us to tangible real estate. When you hand the property over to a property manager, you are giving them day-to-day control of the property, but not the investment. You can still (if you wish) decide which bid to take on the new roof, whether to sell the property and which property manager to hire. Always remember, only one person can manage a property. That will either be you or the property manager. Both cannot do it at the same time.

When you hire a property manager, you will be authorizing them to take care of maintenance issues when they come up. You will have little say on most maintenance issues. Most management contracts, however, do have a non-emergency limit to the amount they can spend on any single item. This amount can range from as small as $250 to thousands.

Finally, trust can be a big issue when hiring a property manager. Let's face it; you are going to be handing over an asset (or many assets) that could be worth hundreds of thousands or millions of dollars. You must find someone reputable that you believe will have your best interests at heart. Trust may be difficult at first.

BENEFITS OF A PROPERTY MANAGER

All the benefits listed below assume that you have hired a competent property manager. Unfortunately, as in most industries, there are a lot of people that present themselves as property managers who are unprofessional and do not know much more, if any, than their clients.

With that being said, the first, not so obvious, benefit of hiring a property manager would be the potential to make more money in the long run. A good property manager understands the ideas of the first seven chapters of this book and has systems already in place to earn you the most money possible. These systems include advanced marketing for your vacancies, economies of scale prices for your maintenance, quality customer service to keep tenants longer, and an understanding of the law to keep you out of trouble. Add it all up over time, and you make more money.

When a landlord has a vacancy, most of them will place a small ad in the classified section of their local newspaper or on Craigslist. They are simply not trained in marketing skills to broadcast their property to a vast audience. Property managers will have the structure in place to get your advertising all over the world. Many of them will have contacts with human resource agencies and relocation companies for various corporations in the area. To become relevant to these agencies, a property manager must have a large inventory of homes. Furthermore, some will have waiting lists of tenants looking for your type of property.

As we noted earlier, customer (tenant) service is vitally important if you want to keep good, long-term tenants. Property managers have the systems in place to take care of tenant needs with little interruption of their daily lives. Keeping your customers happy has the potential to be the most significant financial benefit to you.

Above we listed maintenance as a drawback, but it also can be a benefit. Many property management companies are large enough that they can negotiate with their contractors for better rates for common repairs, passing these savings on to the landlord. Others will have in-house maintenance employees to help further reduce costs to the owners.

A property manager is the best headache relief on the market for a landlord. The day-to-day complaints, confrontations, maintenance requests, collections, evictions, noise complaints, violation letters from a city or homeowners association, and everything else, are better handled by trained and experienced property managers. Little things that would be a problem for many of us to scramble around to find the right person to take care of it is easy for a property manager who has the right systems in place.

As we noted earlier in this book, legal issues have the potential to be a huge problem, even if you do not know it. A good property manager is well versed in the laws and regulations with which you must comply as a landlord in your area. Keeping your business in compliance is one of the biggest benefits of hiring a good property manager.

Preventing problems before they happen is an essential tool in a property manager's box. They have the experience to see what is coming and, many times, keep bad things from happening. They will effectively screen prospective tenants, to ensure you get quality tenants and avoid the ones who will cause you problems.

The most significant benefit of an experienced property manager, however, is the time this person will save the landlord. Time is the most valuable asset any of us have. The more you can save, the more you can do. You can choose what to do with that extra time — take a vacation with the family, find more properties to purchase, improve your career performance, go back to school, or just sit down and enjoy a good novel.

HIRING THE RIGHT PROPERTY MANAGER

As you can see, a property manager has to know a lot of things. It is essential to hire a competent one. If you know someone who is currently using a property manager, ask them if they are happy with them. If they say no, ask why. Their dissatisfaction could stem from a simple misunderstanding or differing expectations. If they say yes, ask why as well, and get the property managers contact information. With trust being so hard to find, a good referral may be your best option. Keep in mind, however, what works for one landlord may not work for another. It is crucial that your business practices can fit into the property management system.

If you do not know someone happy with their property manager, beware of conducting a general internet search for property managers. Admittedly, those that appear high on a search most likely have invested in their business, but as with all internet activity, be skeptical. They could be scammers as well. Start your search at www.NARPM.org, the website for the National Association of Residential Property Managers. This organization is a trade association for scattered site property management owners. From there, look for those property managers who have invested in their education by receiving the Master Property Manager (MPM) or Residential Management Professional designations

(RMP).

When interviewing a property manager, ask for at least three references from current and past clients. If they struggle to find you three, there may be a problem. After getting the references, contact them. You would be surprised how many people overlook this valuable step.

Not all good property managers are alike. They will have different procedures and policies that work best in their company. One may not be better than another. They are just different. Choose a property manager that fits well with your rental business. When interviewing them, make sure they know (and comply with) the laws, demonstrate a priority for servicing your customers (tenants), conduct effective screening procedures, and can efficiently market your vacancies.

The bottom line: listen to your gut. You need to be able to trust your property manager with a substantial amount of money and potential liability. If it just does not feel right, move on.

WORKING WITH A PROPERTY MANAGER YOU HAVE HIRED

Once you have committed to a property manager, step out of the way and let them do their job. They will ask you for all of your documentation, contact information of the tenants, keys, etc. Promptly get the items requested to them. The sooner you do, the sooner life gets more comfortable for you.

Listen to their recommendations. A property manager is not always right, so it is okay to debate an issue with them. Remember, however, that they do have the benefit of education, experience, and market knowledge. If they have made a recommendation to you, chances are you should heed it.

One thing I liked about Ronald Reagan was the way he handled the Soviet Union with his philosophy of "trust but verify." "Trust but verify" can be applied to working with your property manager as well. You should receive a statement from them at least once a month. Go through it carefully, and look for inconsistencies. Remember, they are running their business on very thin margins, so they have to have a lot of clients to make it work. They will occasionally make mistakes. When you see one, call them on it. If you see errors regularly, however, it may be time to find another property manager.

If you happen to hire the wrong property manager, it is not the end of the world. Their contract is usually for less than 24 months. If you are not happy, fire them and get another.

CHAPTER 8 SUMMARY

- Drawbacks to hiring a professional property manager

  o   Cost

  o   Control of the investment

  o   Maintenance issues

  o   Trust

- Benefits of hiring a property manager

- Potentially more income

- Better marketing abilities

- Higher level of customer service to your tenants

- Better able to reduce maintenance costs

- Fewer day-to-day headache

- Less chance for legal trouble

- Prevention of problems before they happen, especially with quality screening

- Increased time for the landlord to spend on other activities

- Get a good referral for a property manager

• Ensure that the property manager you hire is a member of NARPM

• Contact at least three references from the property manager you wish to hire

• Once you have hired a property manager, get out of their way and let them do their job

• Scrutinize each statement from your property manager; "trust but verify."

• Evaluate the relationship, and if it is not going well with your property manager, fire them as soon as you can

EPILOGUE

B rian and Freda have been married for more than 20 years.
They first met each other at a real estate workshop. They
both remember that fateful event fondly, but recently realized they never
put the information they learned to work.

"You know, we've done pretty well for ourselves," Freda said.
"Maybe it is time we invest in a rental house."

"What about Bobby and Jessica?" Brian asked. He was concerned
about their two children. Jessica was in college, and Bobby would
graduate from high school this year.

"We have funded their education over the years," said Jessica.
"Besides, it looks like Bobby will get the same scholarship as Jessica
did."

"How much do we have in savings?" Brian asked.

"Over and above the education savings accounts and our 401K's,
we are sitting on about $35,000 now," she said.

"Maybe it is time to invest in a rental house," Brian said. "It's been
a long time since I studied any real estate. What should we do first?"

"Let's call Monica," Freda said, referring to the Realtor who sold
them their home.

"Good idea," Brian responded, as Freda pulled her new iPhone

X out of her purse. Tapping on her contacts app, she started typing "M-O-N" into the search field and, sure enough, Monica's contact information appeared. After tapping the screen again, she put the phone to her ear and soon heard Monica answer.

"Hello Monica, this if Freda Leftwich," she replied. "You sold Brian and me a house on Plantation Drive about six years ago."

"Oh, hi Freda," she responded, obviously struggling to remember. "How do you like your house?"

"Oh, we still love it, but we are about to have an empty nest," said Freda.

"So, you are ready to move, are you?" Monica said, now genuinely interested.

"No, not exactly," said Freda. "Brian and I were thinking about buying a rental house."

"That's a great idea!" she said. "I own a couple of rentals myself. It is a great source of extra income."

"We really don't know where to start, and we thought you might be able to steer us in the right direction," said Freda. "We need to know where to buy, how much the rent we could expect, what to look out for, things like that."

"I can absolutely help you with that," Monica said. "Actually, I'll do you one better. Let's schedule a meeting with my property manager. That way, we can all put our heads together and find you the right property."

"What's a property manager?" Freda asked.

"He's the person that makes sure the property gets rented and collects the rent for you," said Monica. "He'll also be the expert when it comes to deciding how much rent we think the house will bring."

"Oh, good idea," Freda said. "When can we do that?"

"I have tomorrow afternoon open," Monica said. "Could we meet then?"

After silently checking that appointment time with Brian and getting a positive response, Freda said, "That would work fine."

"Okay, let me check with Geoffrey, the property manager, and make sure he is available," Monica said. "Can I call you back at this number?"

"Yes," Freda said. "We'll wait to hear from you."

"It was so good of you to think of me!" Monica said. "I'm looking forward to helping you with your next real estate venture."

After only 12 minutes, Brian and Freda heard the "The Pink Panther" ring tone coming from Freda's purse. Picking up her phone, while Brian rolled his eyes, she said, "Hello?"

"Hey Freda, it's Monica again," she said. "We are all set for tomorrow afternoon. Meet me at my office at 2 p.m."

"That sounds great," Freda said.

The next morning, Brian and Freda arranged to leave work early and meet for lunch before they met with Monica. After sharing a couple of sub sandwiches and soft drinks, they headed downtown to Monica's office. Upon arrival, the first thing they noticed was the large LED sign displaying the upcoming Sunday open houses for "Your Home Realty," along with a listing of the agents and their headshots. They could not help but notice Monica's picture as it scrolled by as the sign announced that she would be at "Meghan's Retreat" subdivision that weekend.

"Hello, we are the Leftwitches," Bobby said to the receptionist. "We're here to see Monica Sellers, please."

The receptionist suggested the couple be seated in the lobby while she dialed Monica's extension.

Less than a minute later, Monica came bobbing around the corner with her arms outstretched, offering a big hug as if they were long lost cousins.

"Brian, Freda, it's been way too long," she said cheerfully.

"It's good to see you," Freda mumbled over Monica's left shoulder as they embraced

Monica directed them to her office, were a 40-something-year-old man with salt and pepper hair and wearing khaki pants and a golf shirt stood up they entered.

"Brian and Freda, this is Geoffry Pegen," Monica said. "He is my property manager."

"Nice to meet you," Geoffrey said, as he offered his hand, first to Brian, then to Freda.

"You, too," Brian and Freda said in unison.

"*Monica is one of my best clients,*" *Geoffrey said.* "*She has six single-family houses with me.*"

"*And he makes me a lot of money,*" *Monica said as she turned to Geoffrey.*

"*Keep those checks coming,*" *she continued, and they all had a little chuckle.*

After a rather lengthy discussion, Monica and Geoffrey suggested the best fit for the Leftwitches would be either a small, single-family home or duplex. They anticipated a cost of around $100,000, which would require a 25-percent down payment, and leave them with $5,000 for potential post-sale repairs and allow them to maintain another $5,000 in reserve.

About halfway through their meeting, Geoffrey took his leave, asking them to let him know when they had purchased something. Geoffery's departure left Brian, Freda, and Monica perusing through the multiple listing system for a good buy. After identifying four that looked to be good possibilities, they made arrangements to meet back at Monica's office the next afternoon to go out and look at them.

The first building they visited was an all-brick duplex built in 1969. It had two bedrooms and one bath on each side and looked good on paper. Upon inspection, however, they learned there was a great deal of deferred maintenance. Monica warned them of the potential problems concerning the Environmental Protection Agencies (EPA) lead-based paint rules (Renovate Right Program) on older housing, so they decided against it.

The next property was a single-family house in a working-class neighborhood. It had been built in 1992 but recently updated with a new central heating and air conditioning system. It featured three bedrooms and two full baths with a one-car garage. It was convenient to the interstate and zoned for a top-rated elementary school. This property was precisely what Geoffrey had said would make a perfect rental home in their area. They put a star beside this one and moved on to the next property.

They did not even have to get out of the car at the third stop. Upon pulling into the driveway, they noticed large sections of the brick crumbling at one of the corners of the house. The gutters had pulled away from the fascia board, and the front storm door was dangling from its hinges. They marked a big red "X" on this one and headed to the last one.

Finally, they arrived at the last house on their list. It was a spotless, ranch-style house. The yard was in good shape, gravel was recently spread on the driveway, and the landscaping was well maintained. Also, the price was right. The description stated that it only had 1.5 baths, but it seemed to be an outstanding value. Upon opening the front door, they quickly realized why the house was still on the market. It smelled as if someone was breeding wet sheepdogs while chain-smoking. Holding their breath, they made a quick run through the house and closed the door behind them. Brian, Freda, and Monica looked at each other and shook their heads simultaneously, realizing what it would cost to get that odor out.

They traveled back to Monica's office while discussing the four homes and finally decided to make an offer on the second one. It took

Monica about 30 minutes to put the paperwork together. She advised them that the market was pretty strong at the moment and encouraged them to offer near the full asking price. They agreed to make the offer for full-price and asked the seller to pay a portion of the closing costs.

A few days went by and the negotiations with the seller continued. They finally agreed to reduce their request for the seller to pay closing costs by half. Excited about consummating a real estate sale contract, they told Monica to find dinner for himself because they were going out to celebrate.

"What do you think?" Brian said, feeling a little buyer's remorse.

Looking across the restaurant's dining room table at him, Freda said, "It's going to be great! You'll see."

"I know, I know," said Brian. "It's just a big commitment, and we are using all of our savings."

"No, we're not," said Freda. Remember, we are setting aside $5,000 for emergencies."

"Yes, that does make me feel much better, but it's still a big deal," Brian said.

"We'll be fine," Freda said with excitement in her voice. "I'll call Geoffrey in the morning and get him ready."

After jumping through all the hoops and paperwork for the mortgage company, the Leftwiches finally made it to the closing day. They sat in a small conference room of a local real estate attorney and signed an imposing stack of documents.

"Did we just sign a treaty with the Axis nations or buy a house?"
Bryan asked sarcastically.

Geoffrey met them at the property that afternoon.

"It looks like it's in great shape," he said after walking through the house. "I don't see anything that needs to be done before you rent it. You picked a great house."

"Thanks," Brian said. "I think we got lucky. Can you rent it?"

"Absolutely!" Geoffrey offered. "I'll take some pictures for our internet listings and put the sign up today. I can't make any promises, but I believe we'll have a qualified applicant by the end of the week."

"That sounds great!" Freda replied. "Please keep us posted."

Nervously, they drove away, headed for home.

Two days later, after showing the unit to three different prospects, Geoffrey emailed Freda to let her know they had received an application on the property, and that they would start processing it right away.

Two more days went by with no communication from Geoffrey. Brian and Freda began to get nervous again. Freda heard "The Pink Panther" come from her purse, so she picked up her phone and said, "Hello?"

"Hey Freda, this is Geoffrey," he answered.

"Did you rent the house?" she asked.

"Unfortunately not yet," he replied.

"But we received an email saying you had an application on it,"

186

she said.

"Yes, that is the reason for my call," Geoffrey said. "During the background check, we discovered some things that would not be conducive for a quality tenancy, so we had to turn them down. Don't worry; we still have a lot of interest."

"Oh, I'm not worried," Freda said. "I'm sure you are doing all you can do."

"Yes, mam," Geoffrey said. "I just wanted to let you know."

After they hung up, Freda said to Brian, "They had to turn down the application on the house."

"Good thing we had them to discover the tenant might have been a risk," Brian said.

"Good point," Freda said. "I had not thought of it that way. I was just disappointed that the house was not rented yet."

"That's the reason we hired Geoffrey," he said. "He's just doing what he promised."

"You're exactly right," she agreed.

"I love to hear you say that," Brian said with a smirk.

The weekend came and went. Monday morning, Freda received an early email stating they had received another application on the property. This time she did not let herself get too excited about it.

The next day, she again heard "The Pink Panther" ringtone from her phone. Freda noticed Geoffrey's number on the caller ID. Dejected, *she answered.*

"Good news!" said Geoffrey. "We have found a good applicant for your house. They will be moving in on Friday."

"That is great news," Freda said.

"Even better — it brought $50 more than I expected," he said.

"Awesome! I'll let my husband know," Freda said.

Brian was as excited as Freda, but a little more realistic.

"What happens now?" he asked.

"I don't know," she said. "I guess we wait. I remember Geoffrey saying something about being ready for maintenance during the first 30 days of a new tenancy. I guess he will let us know."

Sure enough, the following Monday, they received a small list of repairs requested by the new tenants in their email. After reviewing it, they realized nothing was unreasonable and approved the repairs.

The next year went by very smoothly. There had been three more maintenance requests by the tenants, none of which were unreasonable. The tenants had paid the rent on time every month. They received a notice in their email from Geoffrey informing them that the lease was almost up, and he wanted to make sure they still wanted to continue renting it. Freda asked to do a walkthrough on the house. Geoffrey and the tenants were happy to oblige.

The walk through went great! The house was cleaner than their own. Any concerns they had immediately went away. They signed a new lease with the tenants and looked forward to another successful year.

I wish I could tell you that if you follow all of the advice in this book that you would have no problems in the rental business, but that simply would not be true. The fact is, this is a people business. Landlords are people and tenants are people. When you deal with human beings, eventually, there will be problems.

Do not let these obstacles get you down. A problem is just an opportunity to help someone, or, in some cases, set them on a different path. Either way, it is just something to get through and move on.

Following these guidelines, however, should make you more money in the long run and help you avoid many problems that plague other landlords. Performing a thorough background check on prospective tenants will prevent most problems. Follow this up by treating your new tenants like customers and train them in your style of business.

Do not worry too much about maintenance requests. These are opportunities to improve the property and display excellent customer service, enhancing your reputation in the tenant community. Quality management and proper maintenance can phenomenally increase the income and value of the property.

Finally, if you still need a little help or advice, reach out to your local trade associations. Typically, the people at The Real Estate Investors group or the local association of Realtors are more than helpful. If there is not a real estate investors club in your area, start one. Getting together and talking problems through with fellow landlords not only helps correct issues, but it is also therapeutic.

I wish you great success in building great wealth in real estate.

Happy Landlording!

CPSIA information can be obtained
at www.ICGtesting.com
Printed in the USA
LVHW050348081021
699876LV00002B/3

9 781735 260709